TWILIGHT OF THE ROMANOVS

TWILIGHT OF THE ROMANOVS

A Photographic Odyssey Across Imperial Russia 1855–1918

Philipp Blom & Veronica Buckley

With 360 illustrations, 114 in color

 Thames & Hudson

CONTENTS

Introduction

I love thee, city of Peter's making
I love thy harmonies austere.

With the fishermen I became friends
Often I sat together with them ...
Carefully listening to their tales of the sea.

...the mother of Russian cities is Kiev.

Like a sweet song from my homeland
I love the Caucasus.

*I was impressed by the vast, untapped resources of
Central Asia, which I was seeing for the first time.*

*It was the infantile regime under which we had been living for some
years past, not Russia, not the Russian army, that had been beaten.*

*It was only my passionate longing for resurrection, rejuvenation
and a new life that gave me the strength to wait and to hope.*

Workers? A working class? I know of no such class in Russia.

Once you've grown accustomed to Moscow, you'll never leave it again.

I love my country, but with a strange love…

I love – I know not why – the cold silence

of her plains, the swaying of her boundless forests,

her flooded rivers, wide as the seas;

I love to gallop along a country track in a cart…

To come upon the scattered lights of sad villages,

Flickering in the distance…

I love the wispy smoke of the burnt stubble-field,

the string of carts standing in the steppe at night,

and a couple of birches, gleaming white in the yellow

cornfield on the hill.

With a pleasure unknown to many I see

a well-stocked barn, a cottage covered with thatch,

a window with carved shutters.

And on a holiday, one dewy evening,

I am ready to watch until midnight the dance,

with its stamping and whistling,

to the hum of drunken peasants' voices.

MIKHAIL LERMONTOV, *My Country*

Previous page: The people of a White Russian village celebrate Whitsun, 1916. In their midst, a drunken old man dances to the music. Picture postcard.

Right: Russian Orthodox priests and worshippers, *c.* 1900. The Russian Orthodox Church follows the Byzantine rituals of the Eastern Orthodox churches that arose after the schism of 1054 between the Roman Catholics of the West and the primacy of the Patriarch of Constantinople in the East. Over the course of history, these churches distanced themselves from Western Christianity and played a leading role in shaping Russian culture. The growth of the Russian Orthodox Church was also strongly influenced by its dependence on the Tsarist autocracy. Photograph.

Overleaf: Anton Chekhov (holding a book), together with the cast of his play *The Seagull* at the Moscow Arts Theatre in 1899. The director Konstantin Stanislavski is seated next to Chekhov, Olga Knipper-Chekhova (Chekhov's wife) is standing on Stanislavski's left and Vsevolod Meyerhold is seated on the far right.

THE EXTENT OF THE EMPIRE

For a thousand years…we have been swallowing up non-Russian peoples.
As a consequence the Russian Empire is a conglomerate of nationalities.

COUNT SERGEI WITTE, Premier of Russia, *The Memoirs*

I went to Russia to find arguments against representative
government, and came back a firm supporter of it.

MARQUIS DE CUSTINE, *Letters from Russia*

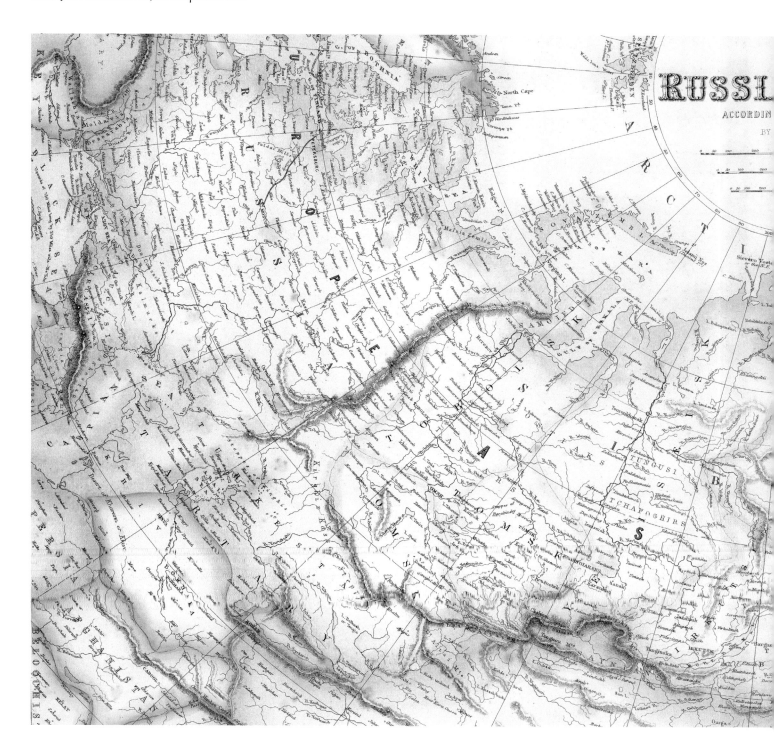

Is autocracy still appropriate, given the character of the Russian people and their state of development? Many clever people have hesitated to pronounce on this, but it does seem clear that autocracy is no longer compatible with the vast extent of Russia's territory, the diversity of its peoples, its economic development…. Whatever the intrinsic merits of tsarist autocracy, it is a geographical anachronism.

MAURICE PALÉOLOGUE, French Ambassador, 15 January 1915

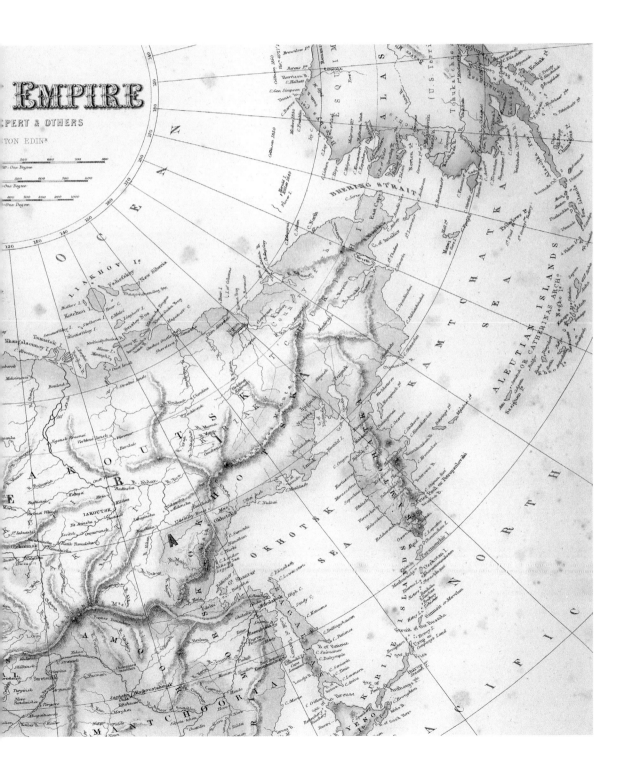

The Russian Empire.
From *The Royal Illustrated Atlas of Modern Geography*, A. Fullarton & Co. Edinburgh, London and Dublin, 1872, pl. VI.

MAP   13

IMAGES OF A VANISHED WORLD

Out there on the crook-backed plain...
where the pitiless eyes of your frenzied
taverns hover above a chain of hills,
staring out of the night into my soul,
where the fatal train of death and sickness
rides – vanish, vanish into the distance,
oh Russia, my Russia!

Andrei Bely

Dare I cast a stone at you? Shall I
condemn your wild and passionate
flame? Shall I not humble myself before
you with my face in the mud, bless
the print of your naked feet, you
homeless, wanton, drunken Russia –
fool of Christ!

Maximilian Voloshin

Kirillov on the northern Dvina Canal. Farm girls carrying bowls of berries. Three-colour photograph by Sergei Prokudin-Gorsky, from the album *Views along the Mariinsk Canal and River System*.

A stout amir in Samarkand, looking challengingly into the camera, three earnest Ukrainian peasant girls, a boy leaning on a garden gate like Huckleberry Finn, a patch of grass with vivid summer flowers – all intensely present, in nuanced colours, true to life, in the world of their own everyday. And if the people in these pictures are long dead and the flowers have long since faded, the cities and landscapes captured here also present a very different aspect today.

The breathtaking original colour photographs were taken between 1900 and 1915 with a specially designed camera by the Russian photographer Sergei Prokudin-Gorsky. The world he recorded on these plates, the Russian Empire, was soon to be destroyed and, in the ensuing blood-soaked decades, rendered unrecognizable. His photographs are snapshots of a vanished world. At the same time, they reveal a surprising continuity: despite the cataclysm, faces, postures, buildings and landscapes still resonate with those who see them, a century and more later.

The photographic journey undertaken in this book is geographical rather than chronological. We wanted to explore this enormously diverse Empire, covering a sixth of the Earth's surface, using contemporary photographs as eyewitnesses, as it were, and setting them in their cultural and historical context. So the journey begins in St Petersburg, established as the Empire's capital by Peter the Great, leads via the northern and western regions to the oriental southwest, continues over the steppes to the Far East, then swings back through Siberia and the Urals to the cities of the Golden Ring near Moscow, coming to an end in the new capital of the emerging Soviet Union. Our companions on this journey include the Scottish photographer William Carrick, Americans George Kennan and Murray Howe, the German–Russian Carl Bulla, Sergei Prokudin-Gorsky, the writer Leonid Andreyev and even Anton Chekhov, together with many anonymous others. Through their eyes we discover a world of exceptional diversity, seemingly timeless, almost archaic, marked by persistent poverty, yet also abundantly rich and often surprisingly modern.

The conflicting impressions left by the photographs are particularly appropriate for the situation in which the Russian Empire found itself in the second half of the nineteenth and the early twentieth centuries. For Europeans especially, it is not easy to understand that immense world, both medieval and modern, both European and Asian. The West's image of its neighbour was long marked by the European bourgeoisie's love affair with Russian culture, notably the novels of Tolstoy and Dostoevsky, but also those of Turgenev and Pushkin, the music of Mussorgsky, Tchaikovsky and the young Stravinsky, and perhaps too philosophers and mystics such as Vladimir Solovyov and Pavel Florensky. According to Isaiah Berlin, Russia appeared to the West to consist of 'nothing but the heavy boot of government on the one hand and the dark, heaving, brutish peasant masses on the other'.

Generations held to this romanticized image of 'the Russian soul', an image only destroyed by the brutality of the Soviet regime. But Russian life and culture had always been much richer, more fractured and more fascinating. Even the Russians themselves could not agree on the nature or the orientation of their own vast land. From the reign of Peter the Great (1682–1725), the battle lines had been drawn between 'Westernizers' and 'Slavophiles'. The former followed Peter in his determination to modernize the Empire and catch up with the culture and economic development of Europe, while the latter held to a vision of Russia as equally Asian and European, a land whose Orthodox piety and submissiveness to fate had given it, culturally and mystically, a uniquely individual character.

From the geographical point of view, at least, the Slavophiles had strong arguments on their side, as a glance at a map of the Empire will show. On the eve of the Revolution, it reached from Poland to Japan and from the Arctic Ocean to the borders of Turkey, the Himalayas and China. With its gigantic steppes, the endless breadth of Siberia, the massive mountain ranges of the Caucasus and the Urals, the Empire was decidedly more than just European. Yet the same geographical diversity created a different problem for the Slavophiles, since the ethnic Russians belonging to the Orthodox Church made up less than half of the Empire's total population. Its hundred and more ethnicities, cultures and languages ranged from Poles and Finns to Jews, Moslem Turkmen, Cossacks, Georgians, Kazakhs, Chinese and Siberian animist peoples. How so many varying political realities might be united is a question that was never really answered.

Above: Grand Duchesses Tatiana and Olga with Anna Alexandrovna Vyrubova (on the right, holding a camera), lady-in-waiting and closest confidante of Tsarina Alexandra Feodorovna, paddling in the surf during a trip to the Gulf of Finland, c. 1914. Photograph.

Below: Russian farm girls, their skirts raised, washing in Derevok, Lyubeshov, Ukraine, 1916. Picture postcard.

In the realm of high culture, too, the Empire mirrored the diversity of its peoples, above all in the challenge to the techniques and traditions of Western culture. 'Slavophile' musicians such as Mussorgsky stood in opposition not only to Western-oriented composers such as Arensky, Tchaikovsky and Rimsky-Korsakov but also to avant-gardistes such as Scriabin and Stravinsky. Alongside the writers, above all Dostoevsky and Tolstoy, who conjured an essential 'Russianness' coloured by romantic ideas and Orthodox spirituality, more experimental voices could be heard: Vyacheslav Ivanov, Leonid Andreyev and Andrei Bely. Other writers, including Gogol, Turgenev and Chekhov, turned a more Western-influenced gaze on Russian (and indeed universal) habits and sensibilities. Philosophers such as Solovyov and Florensky posed as defenders of the Russian soul but even within Russia itself, the more politically oriented thinkers – Herzen, Bakunin, Chernyshevsky, Kropotkin and Lenin – found a significantly larger readership.

The Empire's cultural and intellectual divide was matched by a similar economic and social fissure. Bordered by such powers as Germany to the west and Japan to the east, both of whose societies were drastically transformed after 1850, Russia needed a major industrializing push of its own if it was to compete not only economically but also politically and militarily. After mid-century, hundreds of factories sprang up in Moscow, St Petersburg and other cities, and in the resource-rich areas south of the capital, mines and oil fields were quickly developed as well.

At the same time, however, most of Russia's people were still living in conditions so primitive that, had they been able to read a calendar, they would scarcely have been able to say whether the year was 1910 or 1210. Peasants lived under the same roof as their animals and often at no higher standard. Hunger and epidemics were persistent, and many dwellings were lit by only a single candle that burned before the household icon. In 1880, illiteracy stood at over 80 per cent and few children went to school. Even in 1917, most villages had neither electricity nor running water, no state school, no postal service or police, and even many of the local priests could neither read nor write.

In 1900, there were no more than 10,000 police officers in the entire Empire, most of them stationed in the cities. Beyond the reach of Tsarist law, peasant courts imposed their own rules and often sadistic punishments: an adulteress might be whipped naked through the streets or dragged behind a cart through the village; criminals might be castrated, branded, nailed up, mutilated, hacked to death with scythes or hoisted up and dropped repeatedly until they were dead. Extreme brutality was an everyday occurrence in families too, as witness a well-known proverb: 'The more you beat your wife, the better will the soup be'. In some regions, men received a symbolic whip on their wedding day.

Any rebellion against the provincial landlords would be put down by government 'punishment regiments' made up of criminals, who were free to massacre at will, burning down whole villages and hanging all the local men from nearby trees, ensuring that for some years afterwards there would be no further unrest. The army itself was notorious, and not only for putting down rebellions. Military service for an ordinary peasant lasted twenty years; on leaving his village, the young recruit, nominated by his landlord, would be dressed in a funeral shroud. A soldier's pay was so bad that while he served he was obliged to grow his own vegetables and mend his own boots – it was an army of peasants and cobblers.

Reformers had early seen this archaic state of affairs as the central challenge in any attempt to modernize the Empire and put

Tsar Alexander II (1818–81), c. 1875. Visiting card photograph by Sergei Levitsky, St Petersburg.

it on the road to progress: it was, in effect, a question of catapulting millions of people out of the Middle Ages into the industrial world. The constant argument as to whether the Empire should imitate or reject Western ways had repercussions not only in cultural affairs but also politically: this was particularly so for the period of our photographic journey, from the mid-nineteenth century to the Revolution, a period corresponding to the reigns of Alexander II, Alexander III and the last of the Tsars, Nicholas II.

Each of these rulers represented a different way of approaching the challenge, and also perhaps a different way of failing to master it. Alexander II (1855–81), who regarded himself as a reluctant reformer, was murdered by nihilist students. His successor, Alexander III (1881–94), reacted with a contempt of all progressive ideas, setting Russia back years, if not decades. Finally, Nicholas II (1894–1917), with a fatal mixture of ignorance, indecisiveness and stubbornness, led the Empire directly to catastrophe.

ALEXANDER II

When Alexander II ascended the throne following the death of his father, Nicholas I, in 1855, he inherited not only serious political problems within the Empire but also an armed conflict with the Turkish, French and British (the Crimean War of 1853–56) for control over Russia's southern flank and the territories of the collapsing Ottoman Empire. From this war, which Russia lost, come some of the earliest photographs in this book. Roger Fenton, a pioneer war photographer from Britain, took countless extraordinary pictures of soldiers and battlefields, including a famous photograph of 'The Valley of the Shadow of Death', the scene of the doomed cavalry charge of the Light Brigade. This image, taken after the charge, shows the path strewn with cannonballs.

Russia's defeat in the Crimean War revealed how far the Empire lagged behind its Western competitors, not only militarily and strategically but also economically. It was clear that drastic measures would have to be taken. The conservative Tsar felt compelled to respond, and set in motion an extensive programme of reforms, which culminated, in 1861, in the emancipation of some twenty million serfs. This most important measure of Alexander II's reign was nonetheless beset with difficulties. Many noble landowners, even less reform-minded than their Tsar, refused to make use of new agricultural techniques and implements and as a result soon proved unable to manage their estates without their serfs. Many of them fell deeply into debt and were obliged to leave their lands – a historical development that provided the background for Anton Chekhov's famous *The Cherry Orchard*.

For the former serfs themselves, things were not much better. With their antiquated farming methods, most of them were extremely poor; having no oxen or horses, they often had no alternative but to pull the plough themselves. The land awarded to them as part of the reforms was often of poor quality and the price they were obliged to pay the government for it, a payment lasting fifty years, brought many of them to the edge of starvation. It is consequently not surprising that hundreds of thousands of them sought work in the new factories, although they came as seasonal workers, returning each year to their villages (within Europe, a

habit peculiar to Russia), taking with them aspects of the modern world such as Western clothes and cheap consumer goods. In the 1870s, the Scottish photographer William Carrick documented some of these poverty-stricken workers, caught between city and country. This shuttling back and forth also meant that, unlike the advanced Western nations, Russia retained a peasantry attached to their land and did not develop the kind of real industrial proletariat that the revolutionaries were to depend on for their struggle.

Alongside his programme of internal reforms, Alexander II directed a major expansionist policy in the Caucasus. This aspect of his epoch is also well documented photographically; impressive images of Georgia taken by the American George Kennan reveal a region that, in the 1860s and 1870s, had scarcely altered its age-old social and cultural patterns.

The hesitant reforms, beset by compromise, were not sufficient to unchain the Empire from its backwardness and lead it to modernity, particularly as the landowners were by no means the Tsar's only opponents. In 1881, he was murdered in the street by nihilist students, ironically on his way back from signing a new, liberal constitution.

'The Valley of the Shadow of Death'. Probably the most famous image of the Crimean War (1853–56) shows a road covered with cannonballs, 1855. Photograph by Roger Fenton.

ALEXANDER III

Alexander II's second son and successor, Alexander III, set to
with great energy and decisiveness to turn back his father's reform
efforts and save Russia from 'Westernization'. One of his earliest
official acts was to retract the liberal constitution, a legacy of
the reformers.

The challenges remained immense. Between 1850 and 1900,
the Empire's subjects doubled in number. Industries developed

Left: Tsar Alexander III
(1845–94) with his
family, 1888. In the
centre at the back,
standing next to
his mother, Maria
Feodorovna, formerly
Dagmar of Denmark, is
the heir to the throne,
the future Nicholas II.
Photograph.

Right below:
St Petersburg. The 'Wig
Ball', held on 22 March
1914 at the palace of
Countess Yelizaveta
Shuvalova, during the
last season of balls
before the outbreak
of the First World War.
The ladies' wigs were
designed by Leon Bakst.

and excesses against the Jewish population tolerated or
encouraged by fanatically anti-Semitic authorities. The
most important organ in the authoritarian and reactionary
reorientation of the vast Empire was the Okhrana, the newly
founded secret police, who wielded almost unlimited power.

The photographic record leaves only an indirect witness
of the repressive climate of this era. Although George Kennan
documented the life of political prisoners and exiles on his
journey through Siberia, images from the larger cities present a
deceptive picture of calm, a graveyard calm that pervaded public
cultural and intellectual life as well. Paradoxically, one result of
these repressive policies was a strengthening of the radical

quickly, even if very late compared with the European states.
Nonetheless, by 1890 there were some 1.4 million factory workers
in Russia and the Empire boasted an expanding railway network
of 20,000 miles.

Industrial development, however, remained an isolated feature
of an otherwise largely unchanged way of life. Under Alexander III,
the independence of the universities was rescinded, religious
censorship reintroduced, political persecution intensified, the
Orthodox Church's place in education and politics strengthened

opposition. In 1887, a young Marxist by the name of Alexander Ulyanov, member of an underground organization, having attempted to assassinate the Tsar, was executed. His younger brother, Vladimir, deeply affected by his death, continued his revolutionary work, later changing his name – to Lenin.

NICHOLAS II

Nicholas II, at the age of twelve an eyewitness to the murder of his grandfather, received a rigorously conservative, even reactionary education. His tutor was Konstantin Petrovich Pobyedonostsyev, Ober-Procurator of the Holy Synod of Russia and *éminence grise* behind the anti-Western policies of Alexander III, to whom he served as principal counsellor for more than three decades.

The young Tsar Nicholas, who succeeded the throne at the age of twenty-six after his father's sudden death, was in no way suited to his role. Though his courtly manner and unfailing politeness were acknowledged by all, he was simultaneously stubborn and weak-willed, autocratic and deeply mistrustful of 'Western' ideas. The best that could be said of him by his own Prime Minister, the impressively energetic Sergei Witte, was that he had 'the intelligence and personality of an average guards officer from a good family'.

Nicholas had neither the intellectual stature nor the pragmatic instinct needed to act as absolute ruler of an Empire so torn by conflicts and contradictions. However, it can also be argued that the internal divisions, between poor and rich, medieval and modern, pan-Slavic and Western-minded, were already too extreme for an eventual revolution to be avoided.

Nicholas repressed all 'Westernizing' moves towards a constitutional monarchy, an efficient bureaucracy or any democratic form of government. To combat the undeniable unrest within his own Empire, he relied on the patriotic effects of war and internal violence. The years between 1903 and 1906 were marred by a wave of carefully planned and systematically executed anti-Jewish pogroms throughout the Empire. Tolerated approvingly by the Ministry of the Interior, the pogroms cost the lives of thousands of people. The Tsar himself condemned them publicly but in private revealed his satisfaction with them.

In 1904, Russia's territorial rivalry with Japan in the Far East led to a Japanese attack on the Russian naval base of Port Arthur, and

Opposite above: St Petersburg, a soup kitchen for the unemployed, 1910. Photograph by Carl Bulla. The meal, which was eaten from communal bowls, appears to be *kasha*, a traditional Russian porridge made from buckwheat.

Right: Tsar Nicholas II (1868–1918) and Tsarina Alexandra Feodorovna (1872–1918), formerly Princess Alix von Hessen-Darmstadt, on the occasion of their engagement, 1894. Photograph.

the Tsar declared that in this 'little war' he had found the ideal vehicle for bolstering patriotism within his Empire. Convinced that holy Russia would certainly win a war against 'barbaric' Asians, he ignored advisers who warned him that Russia was not prepared for an expensive war against a modern army. In fact, the troops could not even be properly supplied, since the Trans-Siberian Railway had only one track at that time. It quickly became evident that the Japanese troops were far superior to the Russians, not only in motivation but also in equipment and training, and a Russian defeat was recognized to be only a question of time. With his soldiers lacking supplies and ammunition, an anxious Nicholas had hundreds of icons sent to the front.

The general restiveness that followed this hopeless war was a major cause of the first Russian Revolution, which began in St Petersburg in January 1905 and quickly spread to the whole Empire. Nicholas had allowed his troops to fire on peaceful demonstrators, marching under a banner of 'Long Live the Tsar', who had sought to present a petition to him at his palace. The country was quickly mired in general strikes and conditions of near civil war, which were brought under control only after months of severe repression.

It is not surprising that the photographic record of these last years, the very time that photography became a real mass medium, is the largest and most diverse. Exceptional among these are the original colour images taken by Sergei Prokudin-Gorsky, using a specially constructed camera. Three lenses with colour filters registered the red, yellow and blue spectrums sequentially on a photographic plate, with a fourth lens capturing the image in black and white. These four images were then superimposed and projected as a single picture, though they could not at the time be developed and printed as photographs. When Prokudin-Gorsky moved to Paris after the Revolution, he took his plates with him and they were subsequently sold to the Library of Congress in Washington, DC.

Prokudin-Gorsky had been commissioned by the Tsar to document also the outlying regions of the Empire and to this end he was equipped with a specially outfitted railway car. In a journey lasting ten years, he travelled to dozens of provinces, taking astonishing photographs of Karelia, Dagestan, Armenia, Turkmenistan, Samarkand, Siberia, the Golden Ring (the old 'holy cities' of the Orthodox Church) and elsewhere. From some 700 plates held in the Library of Congress, only a small selection could be reproduced here. A fellow photographer already working in colour was the writer Leonid Andreyev, whose novel *The Seven Who Were Hanged* was to prove an important inspiration in the coming Revolution. Andreyev's evocatively poetic images are mostly of his own family.

Small, portable cameras with short exposure times made it possible for the first time for photographers to record scenes of everyday life. For the German-born Carl Bulla, photojournalism in his adopted homeland became his life's work. Others, such as the American sports journalist Murray Howe, came to Russia for only a short time but nonetheless created powerful images of Russian life far removed from the elegant salons and court ceremonies. The Tsar himself was an amateur photographer and a number of pictures from his family album are presented here, revealing the imperial family in relaxed and intimate mode. At the same time, the album documents the Tsar's lifelong obsession with uniforms; Nicholas felt really comfortable only with his family or when among military officers.

Together, these images, drawn from very different sources, provide a lively and richly diverse portrayal of an Empire unable to establish a stable identity for itself. The vast differences in cultural background and languages and the sudden, disorienting shift into an industrial age made that simply impossible. For us, what remains is an extraordinary treasure trove of faces and stories.

Brought to the brink of collapse by the war, by internal dissensions and by the incompetence of its government, the Empire finally fell in the 1917 Revolution. A new regime began, a regime of cruelty and useless suffering that attached itself seamlessly to the worst excesses of the Tsarist years and for decades far surpassed them.

Typical Russian farming family, sitting round their samovar in front of a wooden house, c. 1910. Picture postcard.

ST PETERSBURG

St Petersburg is not an old city. At the beginning of the eighteenth century, it was no more than a small Swedish fortress and settlement at the mouth of the Neva River on the Gulf of Finland. In 1703, during the Great Northern War which was to end Sweden's long dominance of northern Europe, the area was captured by Tsar Peter I, 'Peter the Great'. In order to expand Russia's maritime power, Peter needed an alternative seaport to Arkhangelsk, on the White Sea, but from the beginning his plans for the new port were far more ambitious. As part of his drive to modernize Russia and increase its ability to compete economically and culturally within Europe, Peter determined to build a new, Western-oriented city to replace what he saw as the backward-looking, over-religious capital of Moscow. The new city was officially founded on 16 May 1703, named after Peter himself.

St Petersburg, described by the Italian polymath Francesco Algarotti as 'this great window in the north through which Russia looks on Europe', swiftly took shape. Having absolute power over every soul in the land, Peter was able to conscript 40,000 serfs per year for the construction work itself. Moreover, he ordered a thousand noble families to abandon their houses in Moscow and elsewhere and build anew in St Petersburg, without any compensation. Forced labour on marshy land in the harsh northern climate cost the lives of thousands of the serfs, earning Peter's great enterprise the unhappy epithet of 'the city built on skeletons'. The enforced migration also drained the coffers of many of the nobles. As the German envoy Gustav von Mardefeld remarked, 'This complies with the fundamental laws of this country, in which everything belongs to God and the Tsar.'

As a meeting place between east and west, St Petersburg has, from its earliest days, been a place of international trade and a centre of artistic and literary achievement. As the capital, it has also been a focus of political strife. It was here, in 1825, that the Decembrists rebelled against the new Tsar Nicholas I; here, too, that hundreds of unarmed civilian protesters were shot down by imperial troops on Bloody Sunday, prelude to the 1905 Revolution; here that the Bolsheviks stormed the Winter Palace in February 1917, forcing the abdication of Tsar Nicholas II and the collapse of the Russian Empire; and here that the October Revolution of 1917 broke out, finally bringing Lenin and the Bolsheviks to power.

By the turn of the twentieth century, St Petersburg's population had reached one and a half million, mainly owing to the growing numbers of rural workers who were abandoning their poor strips of land to seek work in the city. Above this underclass, which generally lived in conditions of appalling squalor and degradation, there was a small but confident middle class, which turned its gaze westwards to Paris and London and whose wealthiest members were richer than all but the greatest aristocrats. The city's elegant Nevsky Prospekt offered a vista of modernist and Art Nouveau façades, while at the lavish Mariinsky Theatre, lovers of music and dance enjoyed regular performances by some of the finest artists of the day, including prima ballerina Anna Pavlova and the great operatic bass Feodor Chaliapin. In 1862, pianist Anton Rubinstein founded the St Petersburg Conservatory of Music, of which the composer Rimsky-Korsakov was among the first professors and the young Tchaikovsky one of the first students. In the mighty shadow of Dostoevsky, younger

Opposite: City of St Petersburg. *Letts's Popular Atlas.* Letts, Son & Co. Limited, London (1883).

Below: St Petersburg. The triumphal arch of the General Staff Building in Castle Square, c. 1904. Photograph.

Reference to Public Buildings (shown red
on the Plan) in addition to those whose
designations are engraved on the Plan.

1 Palace of the Grand Duke Michael
2 Michael Theatre.
3 Palace of the Grand Duchess Helen.
4 Preobrajenski Church
5 British Embassy.
6 Roman Catholic Church.
7 Palace of the Grand Duke Nicholas.
8 Post and Telegraph Offices.
9 English Church
10 Ministry of Foreign Affairs
11 Ministry of Marine
12 Imperial Public Library.
13 Town Hall
14 Great Theatre.
15 Marie Theatre.
Red line indicates Tramways.

Tramways   ...   ...
Public Gardens, &c.
Canals, &c.   ...

literary talents flourished in the city, among them the novelists Andrei Bely and Fyodor Sologub and the poets Anna Akhmatova and Osip Mandelstam.

Apart from a brief interval between 1728 and 1732, St Petersburg was to remain the imperial capital until the Revolution, its Germanic name changed to Petrograd at the outbreak of war in 1914. In 1918, fearing attack by German and Austro–Hungarian forces across the Gulf of Finland, Lenin moved his government to Moscow and the ancient city once again became the capital, this time of the new Russian Socialist Republic.

Left: St Petersburg. View from Admiralty Quay across the Neva River to University Quay, with the Academy of Arts and the Military College, *c.* 1890. Photochrome.

Below: St Petersburg. The Castle Bridge across the Neva, and Admiralty Quay, *c.* 1895. Photochrome.

Opposite: St Petersburg. The island of Vassili Ostrov with its harbour on the Neva, *c.* 1895. Photograph.

I love thee, city of Peter's making

I love thy harmonies austere

And Neva's sovran waters breaking

Along her banks of granite sheer...

ALEXANDER PUSHKIN, from *The Bronze Horseman*

Left: St Petersburg. The Winter Palace, *c.* 1890. Photograph.

Below: St Petersburg. View from St Isaac's Cathedral of the Admiralty Buildings and the Neva, *c.* 1895. Photochrome.

Nature here demands from men exactly the opposite of what they expected: instead of copying pagan temples, they have had to surround themselves with bold forms, vertical lines to pierce the fog of a polar sky, to break the monotonous surface of the damp, grey steppes that shape the Petersburg district as far as the eye can see....
It is up to man himself to build the mountains in this place....

MARQUIS DE CUSTINE, *Lettres de Russie*

Suddenly the first snow began to fall, and it danced and sparkled in lively little diamonds. A bright circle of light from a street lamp illuminated a side of the palace, and a small canal and a little stone bridge. The Winter Canal stretched away into the depths. A smart carriage was awaiting someone there, at the corner.

ANDREI BELY, *Petersburg*

Above: St Petersburg. Quay on the Neva, *c.* 1905.
Photograph by Boissonnas & Eggler, St Petersburg.

Opposite: St Petersburg. Launch of the liner *Bavaldian*
at the Admiralty Dock. September 1901. Photograph by
Carl Bulla.

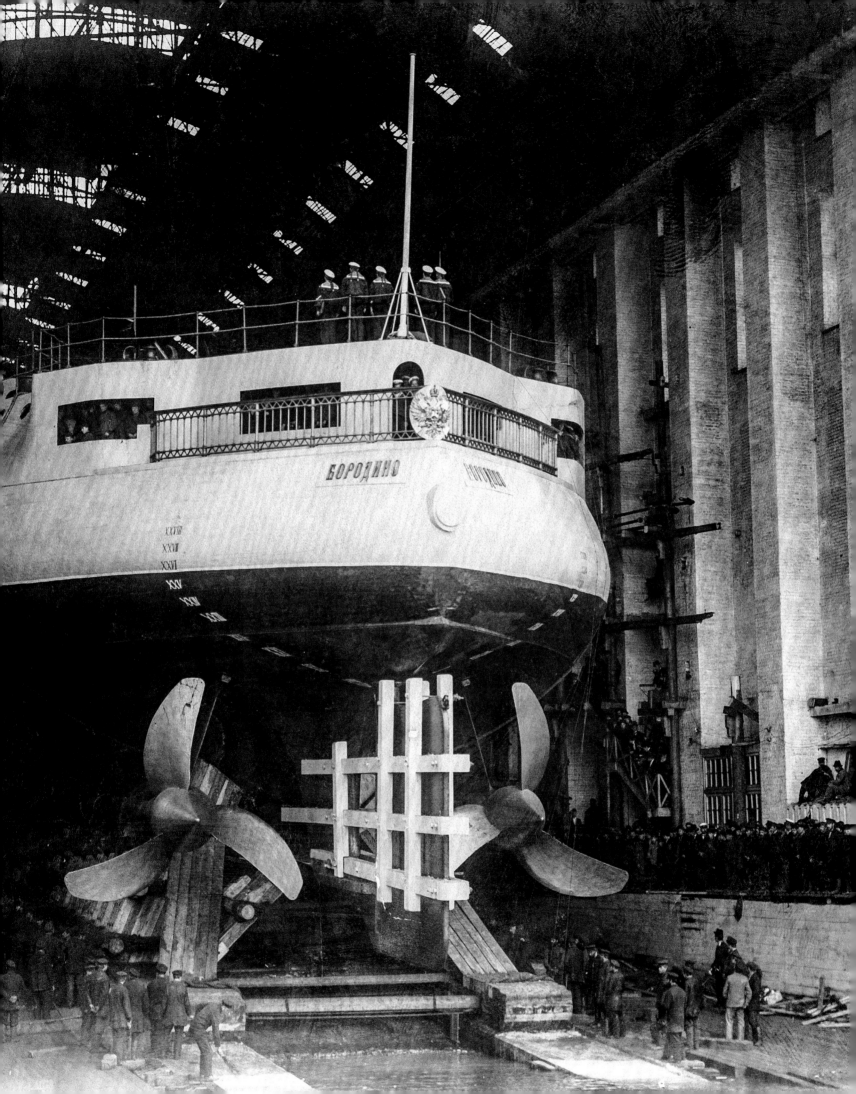

From that fecund time when the metallic Horseman had galloped hither…Russia was divided in two. Divided in two as well were the destinies of the fatherland…. Russia, you are like a steed! Your two front hooves have leaped far off into the darkness, while your two rear hooves are firmly implanted in the granite soil. Do you too want to separate yourself from the rock that holds you…?

ANDREI BELY, *Petersburg*

Saint Petersburg in all her glory and grandeur…The gilded arrow of the Peter and Paul fortress, gleaming in an oppressive sky. The lofty silhouette of a conquering Tsar, one hand restraining his rearing horse, the other stretched out above the Neva….

MARINA DE HEYDEN, *Les rubis portent malheur*

Opposite: Monument to Tsar Alexander III after the unveiling ceremony, *c.* 1909. Photograph by Carl Bulla.

Above: St Petersburg. *The Iron Knight*, a statue of Tsar Peter the Great by Etienne-Maurice Falconet (1782) in Senate Square, with St Isaac's Cathedral in the background, *c.* 1900. Photograph by Andrew Howe.

Below left: St Petersburg. The belfry of St Peter and St Paul's Castle, 1903. Photograph by Carl Bulla.

Below: St Petersburg. Electric trams in winter, with St Peter and St Paul's Castle in the background, 1903. Photograph by Carl Bulla.

There is nothing finer than Nevsky Prospect,

not in St Petersburg at any rate; for in St Petersburg

it is everything. And indeed, is there anything

more gay, more brilliant, more resplendent than

this beautiful street of our capital?

NIKOLAI GOGOL, 'Nevsky Prospect'

Left: 'Aux Gourmets', a delicatessen at 13 Nevsky Prospect, c. 1910. Photograph by Carl Bulla.

Right: The large dining room of the Palkin Restaurant at 47 Nevsky Prospect, c. 1910. Photograph by Carl Bulla.

Above: The first ladies' pharmacy, opened in 1901 at 32 Nevsky Prospect, 1914. Photograph by Carl Bulla.

Opposite: St Petersburg. Nevsky Prospect, c. 1910. Photograph.

Above: The art nouveau cake shop Zhorz Borman at 21 Nevsky Prospect, c. 1910. Photograph by Carl Bulla.

Above: The Parisiana cinema, opened in 1914 at 80 Nevsky Prospect, 1915. Photograph by Carl Bulla.

We spent our mornings at the dressmakers and designers and our afternoons visiting.

MARINA DE HEYDEN, *Les rubis portent malheur*

The old and the new, the liberal touch and the patriarchal one, fatal poverty and fatalistic wealth got fantastically interwoven in that strange first decade of our century.

VLADIMIR NABOKOV, *Speak, Memory*

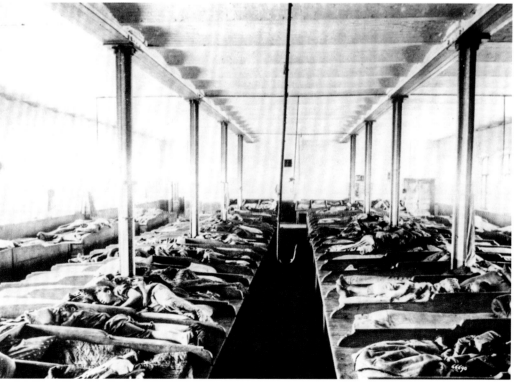

Artists who had won the heart of the public were the object
of warm demonstrations and reaped huge rewards. Frequently
the great woman singers, dancers, and players would find
expensive jewels in bouquets of flowers offered them,
with nothing expected in return.

NICOLAS DE BASILY, *Memoirs*

The boxes of the immense Mariinsky Theatre, with gilded wood and seats of pale blue velvet, formed a perfect setting for bare shoulders. Emeralds, diamonds and rubies sparkled in the light of the enormous chandeliers. The parterre was sprinkled with gold and purple uniforms among the black evening dress.

MARINA DE HEYDEN, *Les rubis portent malheur*

Above left: The actress Vera Komissarzhevskaya, *c.* 1900. Photograph by Carl Bulla.

Above right: Matilda Kshesinskaya (1872–1971), prima ballerina at the Mariinsky Theatre and for a while mistress of the future Tsar Nicholas II. Photograph, *c.* 1910.

Below: St Petersburg, *c.* 1900. The Mariinsky Theatre, commissioned by Tsar Alexander II and completed in 1859. Photograph.

Opposite: Anna Pavlova in Vienna during one of her tours. Anna Pavlova (1881–1931) entered the Imperial Ballet School in St Petersburg in 1891, joined the company of the Mariinsky Theatre in 1899 and soon afterwards became its prima ballerina. In 1905, she gave the first performance of Fokine's *The Dying Swan*, to music by Camille Saint-Saëns, which made her world-famous. In 1909–11, she was a member of Diaghilev's *Ballets Russes* and was frequently partnered by Vaslav Nijinsky. Her uniquely graceful dancing made her a legend in her own lifetime. Photograph by d'Ora, 1913.

Above: St Petersburg, 1903. Religious ceremony in Senate Square to mark the 200th anniversary of the city's foundation. Photograph.

Right: St Petersburg, 1904. Changing of the Guard by a regiment of Imperial Russian guardsmen. Photograph by Carl Bulla.

Opposite: Tsar Nicholas II and his family (from left to right): Olga, Maria, Tsar Nicholas, Tsarina Alexandra, Anastasia, Tsarevich Alexei and Tatiana, 1914. Photographed in the Livadia Palace in the Crimea.

The Tsar is the Lord's anointed, God's envoy as the Church's
supreme teacher and the all-powerful head of the Empire.
In popular belief, he is even the image of Christ on earth.
And since he draws his power from God, he owes no account
of it to anyone other than God.... The divine essence of his
authority also entails the inseparability of autocracy and
nationalism [...] Constitutional liberalism is first and
foremost a heresy, and it is a mirage and an idiocy, too.

MINISTER OF JUSTICE STCHEGLOVITOV, head of the
right wing of the Council of Empire, 19 January 1915

We presented ourselves at Tsarskoye Selo…. The Empress received us in her salon… There were low tables laden with enamel frames and little bells encrusted with precious stones, and a profusion of quartz and jade animals. Pearls and diamonds sparkled on a bed of emeralds in a basket of enamelled leaves.

MARINA DE HEYDEN, *Les rubis portent malheur*

Opposite above: Tsarskoye Selo, near St Petersburg. Terrace in the palace gardens, *c.* 1890–1900. Photochrome.

Above: Peterhof Palace (1723) with its Golden Cascade, west of St Petersburg in the Gulf of Finland, *c.* 1880. Photograph.

Opposite below: Tsarskoye Selo. The Tsar's residence, Catherine's Palace, *c.* 1900. Photograph.

The Court concealed the fact that the heir apparent was a victim of haemophilia, against which all medicine was helpless…. Empress Alexandra…in her desperate anxiety over the illness of her young son Alexei…had placed all her hope in some miraculous intercession, and she had believed her prayers answered when Rasputin, by means which remain mysterious, had twice helped her child through crises that seemed fatal.

NICOLAS DE BASILY, *Memoirs*

It seems to me that the Tsarina made an honest effort to love Russia, but it was a Russia of her own imagination, in which her son was to reign as an autocrat. For the sake of the myth she bitterly opposed the real Russia.

ALEXANDER KERENSKY, Leader of the Provisional Government, *Memoirs*

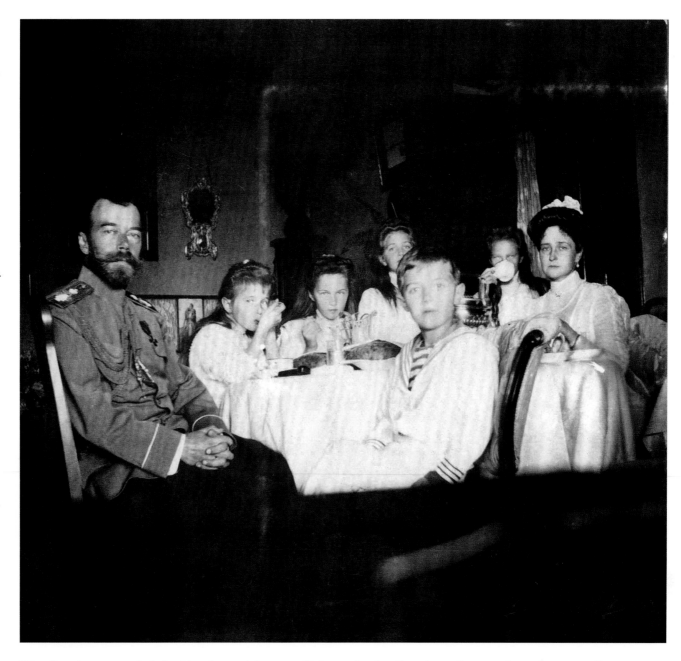

'Until quite recently,' the Tsarina said to me, 'I thought the Russians detested me. But now I see how things are. I know it is only Petrograd society that hates me, that corrupt, impious society that thinks of nothing but dancing and banqueting, and cares about nothing but its pleasures and its adulteries…. But I've been fortunate enough to realize that the whole of Russia, the real Russia, the Russia of the poor and the peasants, that Russia is on my side. If I were to show you the telegrams and letters I receive every day from every corner of the Empire….' What the poor Tsarina didn't know was that [her ministers] were sending her more than twenty letters and telegrams every day via the Ochrana [the secret police]….

GRAND DUCHESS VICTORIA FEODOROVNA, 10 January 1917

Right: Tsar Nicholas II (centre) with the German Kaiser Wilhelm II (front left), in conversation with a senior guards officer in the port of Paldiski, Estonia, 1912. Photograph by Carl Bulla.

Opposite below left: Tsar Nicholas II (centre) arriving in Kiev (Ukraine) on 29 August 1911. Among the reception committee is Pyotr Stolypin (left, behind the Tsar), minister of home and foreign affairs and prime minister from 1906, when, until his assassination in 1911, he was responsible for radical reforms in the Russian Empire. Photograph.

Opposite below right: Tsar Nicholas II with King George V (1865–1936), August 1913. Photograph by Bain News Service.

Right: Tsar Nicholas II and Tsarina Alexandra Feodorovna in seventeenth-century royal attire during the fancy dress ball held at the Winter Palace in 1903 to mark the 200th anniversary of the foundation of St Petersburg. The Tsar's costume came from his ancestor Mikhailovich Romanov (1629–76); it was made of red silk brocade and the Tsar borrowed it especially from the Moscow History Museum. The Tsarina's costume had been worn by Mikhailovich's second wife, Natalya Naryshkina, and was embellished by cabochons plundered from the royal treasury and sewn on to the brocaded coat. Other precious stones decorated the crown, which was based on a contemporary design, while Fabergé himself hastily created a necklace in the antique style, incorporating one of the largest sapphires in the world. This magnificent ball was to be the last great social event in Imperial Russia. Photograph, January 1903.

Left: Tsarevich Alexei on the terrace of the summer residence in Livadia, Crimea, *c.* 1910. Photograph.

Below: Snapshots of the royal yacht *Standard* on a page of one of the Tsar's photo albums, *c.* 1912. Photographs.

Opposite: Grand Duchesses Tatiana and Olga, with Anna Vyrubova (on the right, holding a camera), lady-in-waiting and closest confidante of Tsarina Alexandra Feodorovna, paddling in the surf in the Gulf of Finland, *c.* 1914. Photograph.

To find oneself a girl again
Walking barefoot on the beach.

ANNA AKHMATOVA, from *The Rosary*

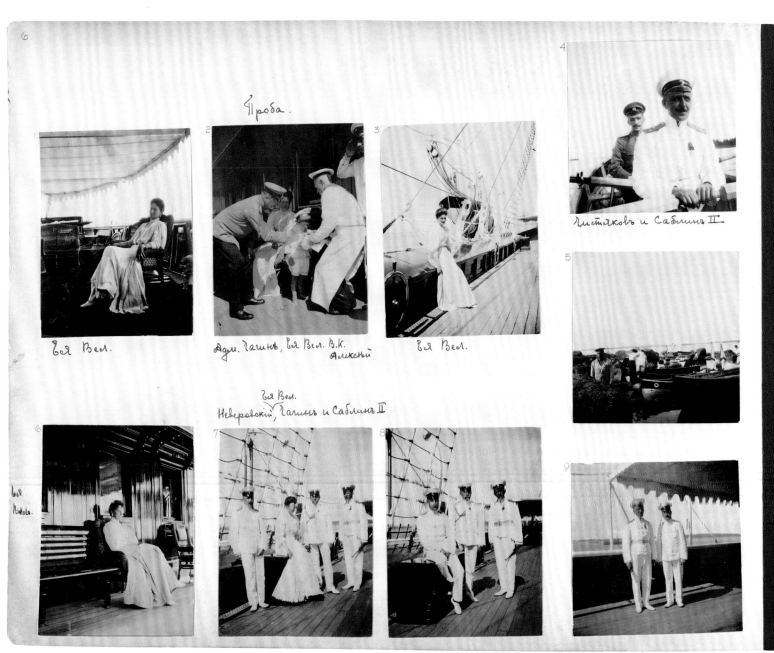

Tatiana's birthday; she is eight years old. We went to church and lunched en famille. We went for a walk; I went in the rowing-boat. It was hot. I read a lot. I killed a crow. We dined at half past eight.

TSAR NICHOLAS II, *Journal intime*

Above: Tsar Nicholas II and Tsarevich Alexei. In his private apartment at Tsarskoye Selo, the Tsar has his photo taken in a Cossack costume, 1910. Alexei is wearing a cap and a fur-lined coat. Photograph.

Above right: Tsarevich Alexei in the garden of the Livadia Palace, Crimea, c. 1910. This was the summer residence of the last Russian Tsar Nicholas II, and was constructed in 1910 to replace an earlier building. It is situated in a suburb of Yalta, on the Crimean Peninsula on the shores of the Black Sea. Photograph.

Right: Tsarevich Alexei and Grand Duchess Anastasia on the terrace of the summer residence in Livadia, Crimea, c. 1910. Photograph.

Above: Grand Duchess Maria in the garden of the summer
residence at Livadia, Crimea, *c.* 1910. Photograph.

My one and only sweetest, You'll read these lines before you go to bed – don't forget, your wifey is praying for you and thinking of you oh so much and misses you terribly.... May God bless you richly and give you strength and wisdom, consolation, health and peace of mind, so that you may continue to carry your heavy crown bravely – oh, what a hard and heavy cross He has laid on your shoulders.

ALEXANDRA to TSAR NICHOLAS II,
Letter of 4 May 1915

Tiring day!...I was terribly wrought up as I went in...to receive the delegations.... (I said) 'I am happy to see here representatives of all classes, come to express their sentiments as loyal subjects. I believe they are sincere...but it has come to my attention that...certain persons have been encouraging extravagant dreams about participating in the management of public affairs.... Be assured that...I will maintain the principles of autocracy as firmly and unshakeably as did my father before me.' We returned to the house at four. I went for a stroll in the garden with Uncle Serge

TSAR NICHOLAS II, *Journal intime*,
17 January 1895, with an extract from his address to the delegates

Above: Tsar Nicholas II and Tsarevich Alexei in hussar uniform, on the Tsarina's terrace in the Alexander Palace at Tsarskoye Selo, *c.* 1910. Photograph.

Opposite: Tsar Nicholas II and Tsarina Alexandra Feodorovna on the royal yacht *Standard*, 22 June 1912. Photograph from albums belonging to Anna Vyrubova.

The Russian people, faithful to the ties of blood that united them with this Slavic nation, raised their voices against the Hapsburg design to humiliate their Serbian brothers. Taking me by the arm, Prince Franz von Hohenlohe, the Austro–Hungarian military attaché in Saint Petersburg, said to me, 'Do you understand that you cannot go to war? If you do, you will expose yourself to revolution and to the ruin of your power.'

NICOLAS DE BASILY, *Memoirs*

Left: St Petersburg. Cheering crowds welcoming the Serbian ambassador, M. Spalaikovich, at the outbreak of war, July 1914. Photograph by Carl Bulla.

Below: St Petersburg. Crowds of people outside the offices of the newspaper *The New Times*, reading the war reports, 1915. Photograph by Carl Bulla.

Right: St Petersburg. Enthusiastic crowds at the railway station, welcoming the arrival of Vladimir Ilyich Ulyanov, better known as Lenin, 16 April 1917. Photograph.

Below: St Petersburg. Demonstration during the February Revolution, near the Tauride Palace, 1 March 1917. Photograph.

Lenin's arrival seems to me to be the most dangerous test the Russian revolution will have to undergo.

MAURICE PALÉOLOGUE, French Ambassador

The disorders had been provoked in Petrograd by a shortage of food supplies, especially of bread. The war had forced the railroads to make an effort beyond their capacity and the result was a growing disorganization of transportation. The inept administration...had not been able to resolve the problem of food supply so important in maintaining order in the capital.

NICOLAS DE BASILY, *Memoirs*

For the past few days there have been disturbances in Petrograd; unfortunately the troops have also taken part.... I went for a walk.... It was sunny. After dinner I decided to leave for Tsarskoye Selo as soon as possible. I took the train at one in the morning.

TSAR NICHOLAS II, *Journal intime*

THE NORTHWEST

Most of the northwest region was incorporated into the Empire in the years between 1703 and 1809. Thanks to Russian victories in the Great Northern War, the two former Swedish dominions of Estonia and Latvia were gained in 1710, and in 1809, following the Finnish War, the Grand Duchy of Finland, which had formed the easternmost third of Sweden, followed suit. However, unlike the Baltic states of Estonia, Latvia and Lithuania, which were under direct Russian rule, Finland retained a large measure of autonomy; the country was not officially annexed and Finnish law remained in place. The Russian Tsar, though Finland's official sovereign, accepted the comparatively modest title of Grand Duke. Attempts to Russify Finland, especially in the later nineteenth century, were unsuccessful, and the historically dominant Swedish culture, rather than being overtaken by Russian, gradually gave way to the native Finnish.

In consequence of these incorporations, the peoples of the northwestern Empire spoke a variety of tongues: Russian itself; Latvian, a Baltic language; the Uralic languages of Finnish and Estonian; Swedish and Norwegian, German and Polish, all with their several dialects; and around Arkhangelsk, the Pomor dialects of northern Russia. Ethnic Germans dominated the middle classes in Estonia and Latvia, where they enjoyed social and political privileges not available to the native people; until 1891, in fact, German was the official administrative language in the wealthy capital of Riga. In Finland, too, German commercial families shared the highest positions with the traditionally dominant Swedes. In Finland and in Russian-ruled Estonia and Latvia, Lutheranism remained the foremost religion, with Russian Orthodox predominating elsewhere.

In every part of the northwest, timber was a vital industry, as well as fishing,

except in Finland. Flax and potatoes were also grown quite widely. It was the timber trade that revived the city of Arkhangelsk towards the end of the nineteenth century. Once the Empire's most important seaport, Arkhangelsk, blocked by ice for five months of the year, had been superseded by ice-free St Petersburg in the early eighteenth century. With the completion of a railway link to Moscow in 1897, the city began to flourish once more.

A direct railway link to St Petersburg was of similar benefit for the fisheries of Murmansk, the very last city to be founded in the Russian Empire. Situated in the far northwest on Kola Bay, it has a sub-arctic climate but remains ice-free throughout the year. For this reason, it was established in 1915 as a terminus for military supplies shipped into the Empire from her allies in the First World War. The following year, though still little more than a railway settlement on the harbour, Murmansk was granted official status as a city.

Thanks to its many lakes and forests, the region became a popular choice for summer dachas for well-to-do families from St Petersburg and even Moscow. The Volga–Baltic waterway, known in Tsarist times as the Mariinsk Canal system, thrusts its way through the northwest, powerfully enhancing the importance of its ports and natural resources. Begun in 1709 and extended over the course of more than two centuries, the waterway is a series of rivers and canals some 700 miles long, linking the great Volga River and the St Petersburg industrial area with the Baltic Sea.

With the March 1918 Treaty of Brest-Litovsk between the new Bolshevik government and the Central Powers, Finland and the Baltic states of Estonia and Latvia passed from Russian control to German. Following the armistice that ended the First World War in November of the same year, all three became independent states.

Opposite: The Russian Empire. From *The Royal Illustrated Atlas of Modern Geography*, A. Fullarton & Co. Edinburgh, London and Dublin, 1872, pl. VI (detail).

Below: A Samoyed family outside their tent, 1905. The Samoyeds are a non-Russian people who originally inhabited various regions of northwest Russia and central and southern Siberia and who lived by fishing, hunting and breeding herds of reindeer. Photograph by Carl Bulla.

Above: The photographer Sergei Prokudin-Gorsky (front right) on a trolley near Petrosavodsk on Lake Onega, 1915. The rail link between St Petersburg and Murmansk, the only port in northwest Russia that is free of ice all year round, was built between 1915 and 1917 in order to safeguard supply lines to and from France and Britain, who were part of the alliance. Three-colour photograph, from the album *Views along the Murman Railway*.

Right: Railway bridge over the Shuia River in Karelia, 1915. Three-colour photograph by Sergei Prokudin-Gorsky, from the album *Views along the Murman Railway*.

Below: Group of railway construction workers on a raft, 1915. Three-colour photograph by Sergei Prokudin-Gorsky, from the album *Views along the Murman Railway*.

I am thrown into life, which carries the streams

Of the race down the stream of decades....

BORIS PASTERNAK

Above: The 84-year-old lock keeper Pinkus Karlinski, who for 66 years was in charge of the Chernigov lock on the Mariinsk Canal, 1909. Three-colour photograph by Sergei Prokudin-Gorsky, from the album *Views along the Mariinsk Canal and River System*.

Opposite: Rafts on the Peter the Great Canal near Shlisselburg on Lake Ladoga, 1909. Three-colour photograph by Sergei Prokudin-Gorsky, from the album *Views along the Mariinsk Canal and River System*.

Above: Arkhangelsk, city in the Northwestern federal district, where the northern Dvina flows into the White Sea. The Sourkof & Chergold sawmill, 1910. Picture postcard (phototype Scherer, Nabholz & Co., Moscow).

Left: Prince Wittgenstein match factory in Siverskaya, near St Petersburg, c. 1895. Picture postcard.

Opposite: Russian bodyguards on an ice yacht in the Gulf of Finland, on the border of the autonomous Grand Duchy of Finland, which was part of the Russian Empire until 1917. Photograph by Carl Bulla, 1900.

Left: Fishing boat and nets in Karelia, 1915. Three-colour photograph by Sergei Prokudin-Gorsky.

Below: Fish smokery in Karelia, 1915. Three-colour photograph by Sergei Prokudin-Gorsky.

Opposite: Fishing village in Karelia, 1915. Three-colour photograph by Sergei Prokudin-Gorsky. All three pictures are from the album *Views along the Murman Railway.*

With the fishermen I became friends
Often I sat together with them
Under overturned boats in the rain,
Carefully listening to their tales of the sea
Secretly believing every word.

ANNA AKHMATOVA, *On the Seashore*

A wide expanse of meadow was already mown and the sweet-smelling hay shone with a peculiar fresh glitter in the slanting rays of the setting sun.

LEO TOLSTOY, *Anna Karenina*

Above: Levshino near St Petersburg. Nuns from the Levshino Convent harvesting hay, 1909. Three-colour photograph by Sergei Prokudin-Gorsky.

Right: Mother Superior on the terrace of the Levshino Convent, 1909. Three-colour photograph by Sergei Prokudin-Gorsky.

Below: The Goritsky Monastery in Pereslavl-Zalessky, near Yaroslavl, 1909.
Three-colour photograph by Sergei Prokudin-Gorsky. All three pictures are
from the album *Views along the Mariinsk Canal and River System*.

Above: Group of children on a slope leading to a church near the White Sea, northwest Russia, 1909. Three-colour photograph by Sergei Prokudin-Gorsky.

Left: Chapel for blessing the waters, in the village of Deviatiny, 1909. Three-colour photograph by Sergei Prokudin-Gorsky. Both pictures are from the album *Views along the Mariinsk Canal and River System.*

Haymaking, 1909. Three-colour photograph by Sergei Prokudin-Gorsky, from the album *Views along the Mariinsk Canal and River System*.

Right: Apparatus for making bales of hay, 1915. Three-colour photograph by Sergei Prokudin-Gorsky.

Below: Karelian men, 1915. Photograph by Sergei Prokudin-Gorsky. Both pictures are from the album *Views along the Murman Railway*.

The institution of communal property is not peculiarly Russian: it is to be found everywhere at a primitive stage in the evolution of landholding. With the development of culture and political organization, it gives way to the institution of private property. But if this process is retarded, particularly by artificial means, as has been the case with us, then the people and the state decay.

COUNT SERGEI WITTE, *The Memoirs*

If you knew how desperately Russian villages
need good, intelligent, educated teachers!

ANTON CHEKHOV

Opposite: Russian farmer and wife, *c.* 1900. Picture postcard (phototype Scherer, Nabholz & Co., Moscow).

Below left: Farmer and son ploughing, *c.* 1910. Photograph by Keystone.

Above: Russian women farmers in traditional costume, grouped round a table with bread and salt, *c.* 1900. Picture postcard (phototype Scherer, Nabholz & Co., Moscow).

Below right: Finnish farmer digging up potatoes, *c.* 1905–15. Photograph by Sergei Prokudin-Gorsky.

Above: Farmers haymaking, 1909. Three-colour photograph by Sergei Prokudin-Gorsky.

Left: Woodcutters on the Svir River, which links Lake Onega to Lake Ladoga, 1909. Three-colour photograph by Sergei Prokudin-Gorsky. All three pictures are from the album *Views along the Mariinsk Canal and River System*.

Opposite: Kirillov on the northern Dvina Canal. Farm girls carrying bowls of berries. Three-colour photograph by Sergei Prokudin-Gorsky.

Above: Sergei Prokudin-Gorsky in a study taken at the Kivach waterfall, the second largest cascade waterfall in Europe, on the Suna River in Karelia, 1915. Three-colour photograph by Sergei Prokudin-Gorsky, from the album *Views along the Murman Railway*.

Opposite: Materiki, near Vologda, about 300 miles northeast of Moscow, northwest Russia. Study of a *dacha* on the waterside. Three-colour photograph by Sergei Prokudin-Gorsky, from the album *Views along the Mariinsk Canal and River System*.

Above: Cornflowers in a field of rye, 1909. Three-colour photograph by Sergei Prokudin-Gorsky, from the album *Views along the Mariinsk Canal and River System.*

Left: At the *dacha, c.* 1905–15. Photograph by Sergei Prokudin-Gorsky.

The sleepy garden scatters beetles
Like bronze cinders from braziers.
Level with me...There hangs a
flowering universe.

BORIS PASTERNAK, from the
series *Beginnings,* 1913

With a sharp and merry blast from the whistle that was part
of my first sailor suit, my childhood calls me back...

VLADIMIR NABOKOV, *Speak, Memory*

I tried to find straw-coloured gloves, but a lady in the shop
warned me that straw colour was no longer the fashion.
I suspect that she told a fib. The truth was she valued the
freedom of her heart too much to risk becoming convinced
of my irresistible attractiveness in straw-coloured gloves.

LEONID ANDREYEV

There, for an instant, the figure of my father
in his wind-rippled white summer suit...
gloriously sprawling....

VLADIMIR NABOKOV, *Speak, Memory*

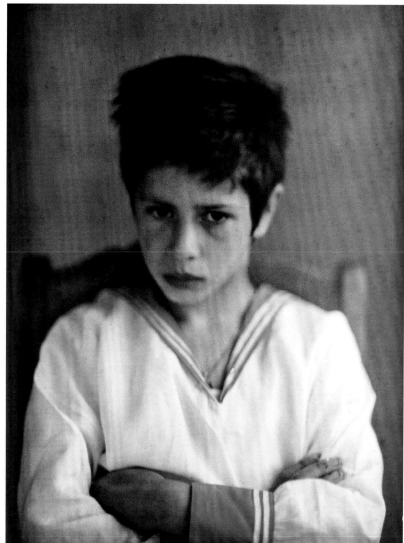

This great urge to work, heavens, how well I understand it. I've never done a hand's turn all my life. I...grew up in a family that never knew the meaning of work or worry.

TUZENBAKH, in Chekhov's *Three Sisters*

Previous pages, left:

The writer Leonid Andreyev (1871–1919) and his wife Countess Anna Wielhorska in the garden of their house in Vammelsuu (Serovo), Gulf of Finland, *c*. 1912. Stereo autochrome from Andreyev's family album.

Previous pages, right:

Above left: Leonid Andreyev on the beach in Vammelsuu, Gulf of Finland, *c*. 1912. Stereo autochrome.

Above right: Vadim, Leonid Andreyev's son, in a sailor suit, *c*. 1912. Stereo autochrome.

Below left: Leonid Andreyev and his son Vadim, after bathing in the nude at Vammelsuu, Gulf of Finland, *c*. 1912. Stereo autochrome.

Below right: Leonid Andreyev's son Vadim with a little girl in a field in Vammelsuu, Gulf of Finland, *c*. 1912. Stereo autochrome.

Left: Lunch party in the summer house of Leonid Andreyev (centre at the back in a white suit) in Vammelsuu, *c*. 1912. The group includes Andreyev's publisher, the architect who designed the house and Ilya Repin (next to Andreyev, in a black suit). Stereo autochrome.

Above: Riga, now the capital of Latvia and a major port on the Dvina River, *c.* 1910. Photograph.

Left: Riga. Railway bridge across the Dvina, *c.* 1890–1900. Photochrome.

Below: Helsinki, Finnish Grand Duchy and part of the Russian Empire from 1809, today the capital of Finland. Quayside, with Russian cathedral in the background, *c.* 1895. Photograph.

Vilnius, capital of Lithuania. Western part of the city on the Vilnia River, 1912. Photograph by Sergei Prokudin-Gorsky, from the album *Views of the Region Covered by Napoleon's Russian Campaign* 1812.

Above: Vilnius. Jewish water carrier, *c.* 1900. Photograph.

Right: Jewish farmers from the area around Vilnius, *c.* 1910. Photograph.

Right below: Vilnius. Old Jewish cemetery, *c.* 1918. Photograph.

To whom shall I tell
my tale of sadness,
Who shall hear my sighs
and my weeping?
You, O Lord, you know
my sorrow, You alone can
take its measure.

Joseph's Lament, from the *Book of Genesis*,
and an Old Russian church song

THE WEST

The western Empire comprised parts of today's Poland, Lithuania and most of Ukraine, as well as ethnically Russian areas and modern Belarus, whose eastern regions were commonly known as White Russia. Peter the Great had gained Ukrainian territories after the Great Northern War between Russia and Sweden (1700–21) and in 1795, the dissolution of the chaotic Commonwealth of Poland–Lithuania had brought these lands into the Empire, greatly expanding its area. The western lands were thus multilingual, as well as multi-confessional, the influence of the Catholic Poles and Lithuanians on the Russian Orthodox population creating a new composite Uniate Church, which, in Ukraine at least, remains dominant today.

The western Empire was also home to the largest population of Jews in the Empire, largely owing to the absorption of much of the former Polish–Lithuanian Commonwealth. The Pale of Settlement, established by Catherine the Great at that time and still in force at the time of the 1917 Revolution, obliged all but a very few of the Empire's Jews to establish permanent residence within the western territories or, initially, some areas further to the south. The predominantly Jewish city of Vilnius, in Lithuania, was even proposed as the capital of a new Jewish state to be founded in the region. Politically and culturally liberal, Vilnius was home also to Polish, Belorussian and Lithuanian nationalist movements. Very few ethnic Lithuanians actually lived in Vilnius, however; most laboured in agriculture outside the city.

Until quite late in the nineteenth century, even Kiev, in the Ukraine, was no more than a provincial backwater on the Dnieper River. A once great city, the capital of early medieval Rus' and one of the oldest cities in all of eastern Europe, Kiev had been largely destroyed in the Mongol invasions of the thirteenth century, and it was not until the substantial industrial development of the later nineteenth century that it rose to prominence once again, the new railways playing a vital part in its growth.

The most important city in the western Empire, however, was Warsaw, which in 1815 had been transferred from Prussian rule to be the capital city of a constitutional monarchy under Russian suzerainty, Russia's Tsar becoming Poland's King. Dissatisfaction with this arrangement led to periodic rebellions during the nineteenth century, but by 1900 the city had enjoyed a long period of peaceful modernization and its population had climbed to some 630,000.

The western Empire was mostly rural and poor, though parts of Ukraine lay within the fertile chernozem (black-earth) belt, with a reliable grain surplus available for export. The export crops of wheat and, later, sugar beet, however, were mostly grown on large landowner estates. Peasants working their own lands grew mainly the traditional rye and oats, with flax and potatoes serving as small-scale cash crops in some areas. After the Emancipation of the Serfs in 1861, wheat production increased enormously, so that by 1910, Russian wheat, much of it from the western region, had risen to some 35% of world export stocks, thanks partly to hardier wheat strains, though not to any improvement in agricultural techniques. Even after the Emancipation, conditions of virtual slave labour persisted and consequently productivity in the Empire continued to lag behind that of western Europe.

Russia's western Empire formed a major part of the Eastern Front during the First World War. Patriotic Poles aspired to a nation of their own that would emerge out of the mutual destruction of Central and Allied powers, many battles having been fought on historic Polish territories. In the winter of 1916–17, German and Russian forces in Vilnius were obliged to call a truce in order to fight off the packs of starving wolves marauding the city.

Like Finland and the Baltic states of Estonia and Latvia, Poland and the other western lands of Lithuania, Ukraine and Belarus passed from Russian suzerainty to German in March 1918, with the signing of the Treaty of Brest–Litovsk between the

Opposite: The Russian Empire. From *The Royal Illustrated Atlas of Modern Geography*, A. Fullarton & Co. Edinburgh, London and Dublin, 1872, pl. VI (detail).

Below: A Jewish *shtetl* (community) in Russian Poland, c. 1900. Photograph.

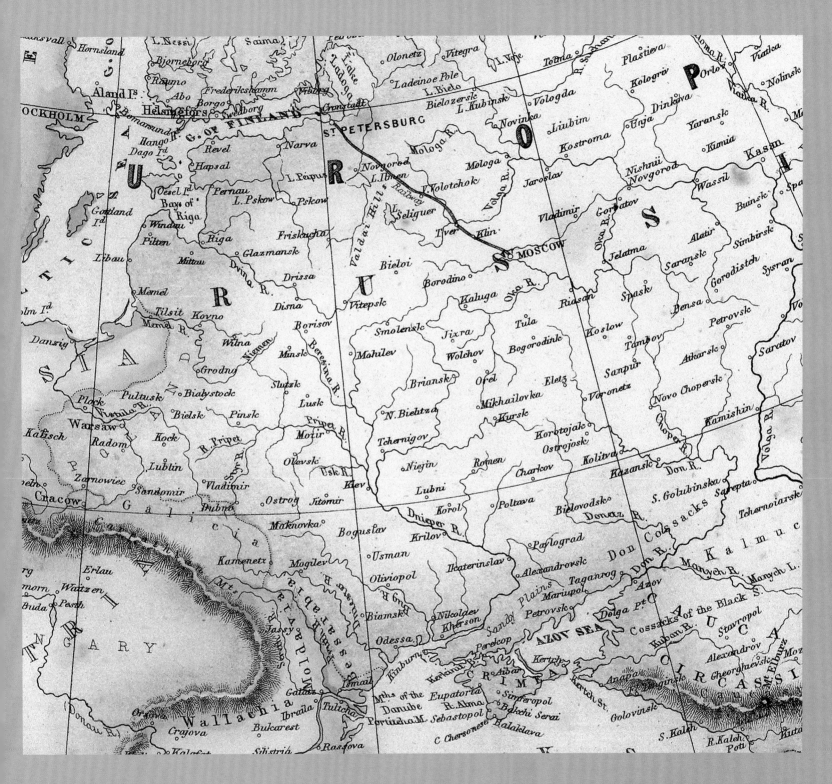

Central Powers and the Bolsheviks. All these territories gained independence with the armistice that ended the First World War in
November of the same year.

Above: Vitebsk, now in Belarus. Cathedral of the Assumption, 1912. Three-colour photograph by Sergei Prokudin-Gorsky, from the album *Views of the Region Covered by Napoleon's Russian Campaign 1812*.

Left: Mogilev, now in Belarus. Theatre Square, c. 1910. Picture postcard.

Opposite: Farmer on his way to the market in Kamyanka, now in Ukraine, c. 1870. Photograph by William Carrick.

Above: Pinsk, now in Belarus. Horse and cart on unsurfaced road, 1916. Picture postcard.

Right above: Voupa, Russian Poland, now in Belarus. The famous wooden synagogue dating from the first half of the eighteenth century, destroyed in 1941 during the Second World War. Photograph, c. 1910.

Right centre: Pinsk. Main street with church, c. 1910. Picture postcard.

Right. Typical East European temple; on the right, separated by a wooden grid, is the 'school for women', c. 1905. Photograph.

Baptism is obligatory for all Russian children, that is, those born to Orthodox parents; the State doesn't view Catholics, Jews, Muslims or Protestants as Russians: they're only non-native subjects....

ANONYMOUS, *Confession sexuelle d'un anonyme russe*

Above left: Jewish street musicians in Warsaw, *c.* 1890. Photograph.

Above: Warsaw, Russian Poland, now capital of Poland. Market scene, *c.* 1897. Stereo photograph by B. W. Kilburn.

Left: Warsaw. Jewish children, *c.* 1897. Stereo photograph by B. W. Kilburn.

Above: Warsaw, Russian Poland, now capital of Poland. Market in a square in the historic old city, *c.* 1890–1900. Photochrome.

Right: Street scene with two beggars and a Russian Orthodox priest in the background, *c.* 1900. Photograph.

Opposite: Warsaw. Russian school and statue of Nicolaus Copernicus, *c.* 1910. Photograph.

I arrived at Kiev about midday on Good Friday....
It was a relief to find hills and a real river.

R. H. BRUCE LOCKHART, *Memoirs of a British Agent*

Above: Kiev, now capital of Ukraine. The Podol quarter, the old trading and harbour area of the city on the Dnieper River, *c.* 1890–1900. Photochrome.

Right: Kiev. The Nicholas Chain Bridge across the Dnieper, *c.* 1890–1900. Photochrome.

Opposite: Kiev. The Kiev-Pechersk Lavra, or Monastery of the Cave, one of the oldest Russian Orthodox monasteries in Ukraine, with its bell-tower in the foreground, *c.* 1890–1900. Photochrome.

This Russian Empire of ours consists of a
multitude of cities: capital, provincial, district,
downgraded...and the mother of Russian cities is Kiev.

ANDREI BELY, *Petersburg*

I 'did' Kiev with all the thoroughness of a typical American tourist.... The fine weather had brought the whole of the town into the streets, Russians doing their Easter shopping and Jew shopkeepers catering for their needs. For in spite of its churches, Kiev is almost more Jewish than Christian.

R. H. BRUCE LOCKHART, *Memoirs of a British Agent*

Above: Kiev. Kreshchatyk Street, the city's magnificent main boulevard, *c.* 1890–1900. Photochrome.

Left: Kiev. Nikolayev Street, *c.* 1890–1900. Photochrome.

Opposite: Kiev. Milkmaids in traditional costume, *c.* 1900. The earthenware milk jugs hang on wooden poles. Photograph.

Above: Children bathing in the Volga, *c.* 1910. Photograph.

Left: Bathers in the Dvina, near Polatsk, now in Belarus, *c.* 1910. Picture postcard.

Below: Russian farm girls, their skirts raised, washing in Derevok, Lyubeshov, now in Ukraine, 1916. Picture postcard.

In Russia, especially in the country, people of all ages and both sexes commonly swim completely naked in the rivers and the sea.

ANONYMOUS, *Confession sexuelle d'un anonyme russe*

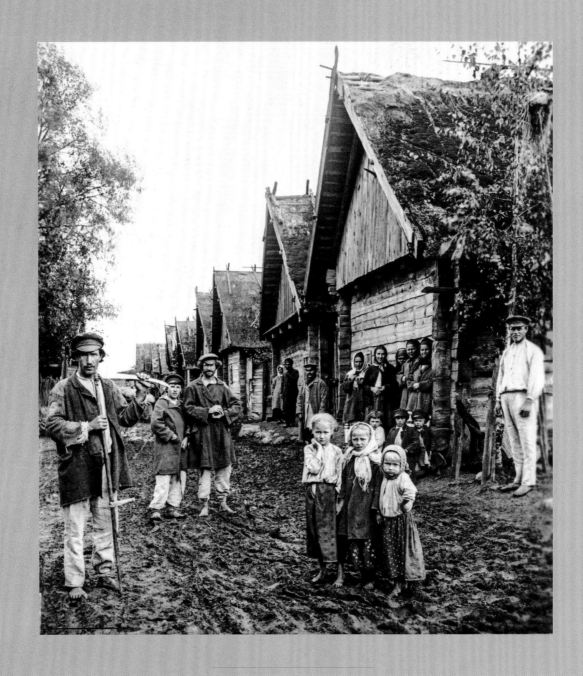

How stale Russia is! Everything rancid, stuffy....

I can't stand Russia! Ignorance, stinking, and instead

of scarves, foul-smelling foot-rags....

GLAGOLIEV, in Chekhov's *Platonov*

Above: Woman farmer pounding grain with a wooden pestle, *c.* 1910. Photograph.

Left: Ukrainian woman farmer, *c.* 1905–15. Three-colour photograph by Sergei Prokudin-Gorsky, from the album *Different Views and Studies of the Russian Empire*.

The peasants are all the same. They're uncivilized and they live in filth.

ASTROV, in Chekhov's *Uncle Vanya*

Opposite: Inhabitants of a Russian village, in traditional costume, *c.* 1910. Photograph.

Right: Farming family outside their house in Derevok, Ukraine, *c.* 1910. Picture postcard.

THE SOUTHWEST

The Southwest was a rich and diverse territory encircling most of the Black Sea and lapping the shores of the vast Caspian Sea. It encompassed southern Ukraine, Bessarabia (eastern Moldavia), Georgia, Armenia, Azerbaijan and several provinces of northeastern Turkey. Few of the area's inhabitants were ethnic Russians; within the Empire, they were officially registered as *inorodtsy* – non-Slavs or, literally, 'people of another origin'. They spoke Persian and a great variety of Turkic and Caucasian languages, and they also included German farmers, descendants of the Mennonite settlers invited by Catherine the Great, and a large Jewish population in the important port of Odessa. Apart from the Shia Muslims of Azerbaijan and the Turkish Sunnis, most southwestern peoples practised a form of Orthodox Christianity.

Russia had gradually expanded its control of the southwest during the late eighteenth and nineteenth centuries, with territories wrested from the Persian and Ottoman Empires and the Crimean Tatars. The long Caucasian War (1817–64) had ended with the annexation of the Muslim north Caucasus, including Chechnya, Dagestan and Circassia, the intractable Circassians being subsequently driven into exile in an early instance of 'ethnic cleansing'. The centuries-old enmity with the Turks, together with the economic importance of the Black Sea separating eastern Europe from western Asia, had provided a major impetus for the Russian drive southwards.

The Black Sea itself was the most important theatre of the Crimean War (1853–56) between Russia and an alliance of the British, French and Ottoman Empires and the Kingdom of Sardinia. Russia had entered the war under the pretext of protecting Christian Ottoman subjects. Defeat cost the Empire the right to station military forces on its long Black Sea coast, seriously weakening its position relative to the Turks. However, a subsequent victory in the Russo–Turkish War (1877–78) allowed Russia to reassert control over most of the Black Sea region, a vital step for the Empire's economic development. Further to the east, the great industrializing push of the nineteenth century transformed the Azerbaijani capital of Baku, with its vast oil reserves, from a useful to a crucial imperial territory. The first offshore and machine-drilled wells in the world were dug here and by the mid-1870s, Baku had become a 'black gold' boomtown; by the turn of the twentieth century, it was the centre of the international oil industry.

The warm climate and natural beauty of Yalta soon made this Black Sea city a tourist mecca for well-to-do Russians. Anton Chekhov built his 'white dacha' in Yalta and wrote several of his great plays there. Commercial Odessa proved even more attractive, if for different reasons, for those with money to spare. Founded in 1794 near the mouths of four major rivers, a free port since the early nineteenth century, Odessa was one of the Empire's largest cities and its most important seaport. Odessa flourished thanks to the wheat trade, which by 1910 had risen to some 35% of world export stocks, 90% of these traded through the city.

The English travel writer Edmund Spencer wrote in 1851: 'Odessa cannot be considered a Russian town with reference to its inhabitants, who are principally Germans, Italians, Greeks, Jews, Armenians, and a few French and English; merchants from every part of the world may be seen wandering about the streets in all the variegated costumes of Europe and Asia, which adds not a little to the gaiety and variety....' Though within the Pale of Settlement, Odessa's overriding commercial ethos encouraged the mixing of Jews with Gentiles rather than their separation; social integration was high, and the Jewish families of Odessa were less traditionally religious and more Westernized than elsewhere in the Empire. This was not

Opposite: The Russian Empire. From *The Royal Illustrated Atlas of Modern Geography*, A. Fullarton & Co. Edinburgh, London and Dublin, 1872, pl. VI (detail).

Below: Yalta, on the southern coast of the Crimean Peninsula on the Black Sea, Ukraine, c. 1895. Photograph.

enough, however, to prevent vicious pogroms here as well as in smaller southwestern towns such as Kishinev, where, in the words of Sergei Witte, 'the most barbarous and disgraceful of these pogroms' took place. Led by Orthodox priests and tacitly encouraged by the authorities, the pogroms served to deflect criticism from the increasingly unpopular government.

On the collapse of the Empire, Georgia, Armenia and Azerbaijan joined forces in a Transcaucasian Federation, which survived only a few months. By the early 1920s, Bessarabia had united with Romania and the northeastern Turkish areas had been returned to Turkey or Georgia, while the remaining southwestern territories had been incorporated into the new Soviet Union.

Above: Odessa. The Richelieu Steps, known since 1955 as the 'Potemkin Steps', after the famous scene in Eisenstein's film *Battleship Potemkin*. The 192 steps link the city centre with the port. Photochrome, *c.* 1890–1900.

Opposite: Odessa, now in Ukraine. The Pushkin Monument (1889) in front of the City Hall. Alexander Pushkin (1799–1837) lived in Odessa for part of the time between 1820 and 1824. Photograph, *c.* 1890.

Above: Odessa. The opera house, opened in 1887, emblem of the port on the Black Sea, *c.* 1890–1900. Photochrome.

Left: The seaside resort of Petite-Fontaine, near Odessa, *c.* 1890–1900. Photochrome.

Opposite: Odessa. View of Pratique harbour, *c.* 1890–1900. Photochrome.

The economic growth of our Southern provinces goes on very rapidly and successfully. We may expect that our Southern provinces will be transformed into a rich industrial region owing to their abundance of iron ore and coal and their proximity to the Black Sea coast. This is bound to produce increased trade through the Black Sea. The development of railroads and the growing exploitation of natural resources in the economic hinterlands of the Black Sea areas...will have a similar effect on the trade.

NICOLAS DE BASILY, *Memoirs*

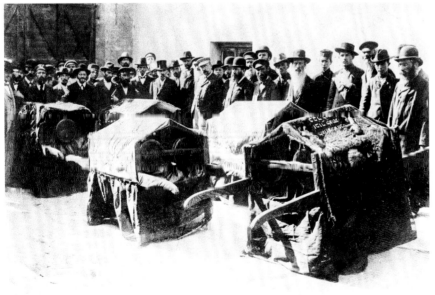

Two Jews came walking, came walking here.
'You Jews, you Jews, you cursed Jews,
You have murdered my son on the Cross.'

Old Russian church song

One of our Orthodox priests assured me that Christ himself was not a Jew, although he was the son of the Jewish God and his mother was a Jew. He admitted those things, but said all the same, 'That could not be.' I asked him, 'So how do you explain it?' He shrugged and said, 'This to me is a great mystery!'

LEO TOLSTOY

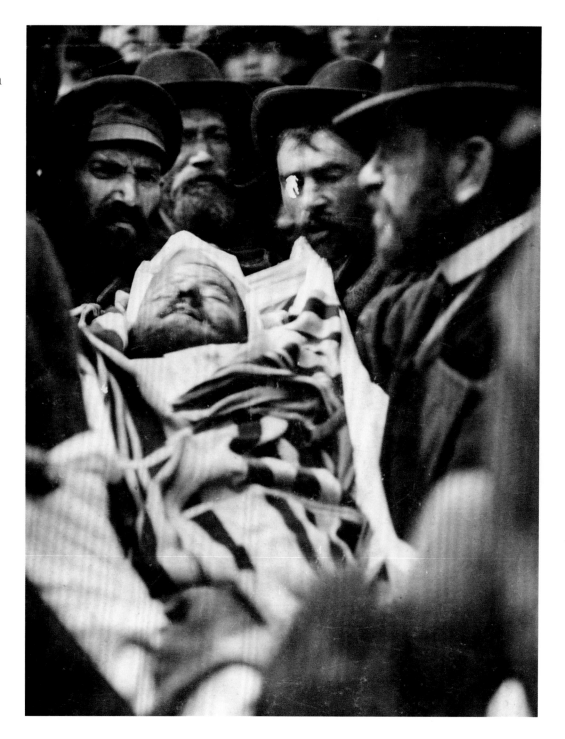

Opposite above: Chisinau, Bessarabia, now capital of Moldova. A victim of the anti-Semitic pogrom. In around 1900, the city was one of the most thriving centres of Jewish life in the Russian Empire. Photograph, 1905.

Opposite below: Chisinau. The Torah scrolls damaged during the pogrom are solemnly taken for burial, 1903. Photograph.

Right: Chisinau. A victim of the pogrom is laid out for burial, 19 April 1903. Photograph.

Into the valley of death
Rode the six hundred...
Cannon to right of them,
Cannon to left of them,
Cannon in front of them
Volley'd and thunder'd...
Cossack and Russian
Reel'd from the sabre-stroke
Shatter'd and sunder'd.
Then they rode back, but not
Not the six hundred.

ALFRED, LORD TENNYSON,
from *The Charge of the Light Brigade*

Opposite above: Crimean War. The British supply port near Balaclava, southeast of Sevastopol, 1855. Photograph by Roger Fenton.

Opposite below: Crimean War. 'The Valley of the Shadow of Death'. Probably the most famous photograph of the Crimean War (1853–56) shows a road covered with cannon balls, 1855. Photograph by Roger Fenton.

Above: Crimean War. An English nurse tends to an injured soldier, 1855. Photograph by Roger Fenton.

In the heat of noon...I lay motionless, with a bullet in my breast. My deep wound was still streaming, and my blood oozed out, drop by drop.

MIKHAIL LERMONTOV, from *The Dream*

The Chechens...lay dead and hacked about. Only one...though wounded in many places, was still alive. All covered with blood...he crouched, dagger in hand, still prepared to defend himself. The cornet went up to him...and with a quick movement shot him in the ear.

LEO TOLSTOY, *The Cossacks*

Russian women are passionate, tender, sensual, but not romantic.... We don't care for French novels with their psychological verbiage and sentimental theories. Our love letters are simplicity itself. Anyway, we're too lazy to write. We never know quite what we're doing, or even what time of day it is.... We wander through life like shadows under the moon.... We have nocturnal souls.

PRINCESS D.

Above: Summer idyll. Three-colour photograph by Sergei Prokudin-Gorsky, from the album *Different Views and Studies of the Russian Empire*.

Right: Summer holidays in the Crimea: the Chernikoffs, an upper-class Jewish family from Rostov on the Don, *c.* 1910. Photograph.

Above: Yalta, in the Crimea, now in Ukraine. View of the port, *c.* 1910. Photograph.

Right: Yalta, in the Crimea. Hotels along the promenade of the spa and holiday resort on the Black Sea, 1911. Picture postcard.

Above: Orenburg, in the Volga federal district, not far from the border with Kazakhstan. Pedestrian bridge across the Ural River. The Cossacks who settled in Orenburg were supposed to create a buffer zone between the Tatars and the Kazakhs and to secure the influence of the Russian Empire – predominant since 1731 – over the Minor Horde, a federation of Kazakh tribes. Picture postcard, 1915.

Left: Rostov on the Don, in the Southern federal district. Panorama of the city, also known as the 'Gateway to the Caucasus', 1905. Picture postcard (phototype Scherer, Nabholz & Co., Moscow).

Right: Cossack horsemen, two standing in the saddle, *c.* 1900. Photograph.

Lukáshka...was a tall, handsome lad about twenty years old.... Though he had only lately joined the Cossacks...it was evident from the expression of his face and the calm assurance of his attitude that he had already acquired the somewhat proud and warlike bearing peculiar to Cossacks...and that he felt he was a Cossack and fully knew his own value.

LEO TOLSTOY, *The Cossacks*

Left: Soldiers doing the *kazachok*, a Cossack dance. The Slavic Cossacks created their own settlements during and after the sixteenth century, and became militarized farmers. During the seventeenth century, they formed the quasi-state of Cossack Hetmanate in Ukraine, which fought against Polish rule and later entered the Russian Empire as an autonomous state. Until the eighteenth century, both Russian and Ukrainian Cossacks were partly independent of the Tsarist Empire, but then they gradually became integrated into the Russian army as free cavalry units. The main Cossack settlements were in the regions of the Don, the Dnieper and the Ural. Ural and Orenburg Cossacks played a significant role in the conquest and colonization of Siberia.

Right: Volga boatman or *burlak* hauling a barge, c. 1900. Photograph.

Although the muzhiks have no education, their intelligence
is quick and supple.... Their minds are always working.
They don't say much, but they're always thinking...firstly
about their material interests, their harvest, their cattle, the
poverty gripping or threatening them, the price of clothes
and tea, the burden of taxes and daily chores, the next agrarian
reform.... But they think of higher things, too, especially
during those interminable winters....

PRINCESS P.

120

Opposite: Russian farmer and family in a horse and cart, 1900. Picture postcard (phototype Scherer, Nabholz & Co., Moscow).

Right: Russian farmers sitting at table with a samovar outside their wooden house; one is playing the balalaika, *c.* 1875. Photograph by Sergei Prokudin-Gorsky, from the album *Views along the Mariinsk Canal and River System*.

Though torn from you by fate, O southern mountains,

In the morning of my life,

To remember you forever

It is enough to have once been there:

Like a sweet song from my homeland

I love the Caucasus.

MIKHAIL LERMONTOV, from *The Caucasus*

Above: Artvin, in modern-day Turkey. During the nineteenth century, both the town and the province on the Georgian border frequently switched between the Ottoman and the Russian Empire. Three-colour photograph by Sergei Prokudin-Gorsky, from the album *Views of the Caucasus and the Black Sea Region*.

Opposite: The Bagatsk Gorge in the Caucasus, *c.* 1890–1900. Photochrome.

Bathing in the...waters strengthens the body and increases animation, but, as I was to learn, too much animation can strain the heart and people were warned against staying in too long.... [The Prince]...was able to stay in the waters a long time and drink a bottle of champagne while in them, all with no ill effect.

COUNT SERGEI WITTE, *The Memoirs*

Left: Borjomi, in modern Georgia, a thermal spa and summer resort in the Lesser Caucasus. Two thermal springs, which in the 1840s were named after General Yevgeni Golovin and his daughter Yekaterina, together with its beautiful scenery, led to the town being called the 'Pearl of the Caucasus'. Pavilion with patients at the Yevgeni Spring, *c.* 1905–15. Three-colour photograph by Sergei Prokudin-Gorsky.

Right above: Borjomi. Bottling plant for the town's famous mineral water, 1905–15. Three-colour photograph by Sergei Prokudin-Gorsky.

Right below: Borjomi. Pavilion at the Yekaterina Spring, 1905–15. Three-colour photograph by Sergei Prokudin-Gorsky. All three pictures are from the album *Views of the Caucasus and the Black Sea Region*.

Above: Baku, now capital of Azerbaijan. Oil fields with derricks, *c.* 1890. In around 1900 the oilfields on the shores of the Caspian Sea were the biggest in the world, accounting for half the world's oil production. Photograph by Dmitri Yermakov.

Left: Baku. Palace of the Khan of Baku, *c.* 1890. Photograph from the Caucasus expedition by Count Jenö Zichy.

Opposite: Dagestan, in the North Caucasian federal district. Landscape with waterfall, near the fortress of Hunsag, *c.* 1890. Photograph from the Caucasus expedition by Count Jenö Zichy.

Caucasians are straightforward people, who act as
God prompts them, and they do not like wiles.

COUNT SERGEI WITTE, *The Memoirs*

Above: Karachay-Cherkessia, in the North Caucasian federal district. Cherkessians from the Karachay
region, *c.* 1890. Photograph from the Caucasus expedition by Count Jenö Zichy.

Opposite: Karachay-Cherkessia. Cherkessian woman from the Kuban region,
c. 1890. Photograph from the Caucasus expedition by Count Jenö Zichy.

Above: Chakva, near Batumi, on the east coast of the Black Sea, now Ajaria, in Georgia. Women from the Greek minority helping to harvest the tea, 1905–15. Three-colour photograph by Sergei Prokudin-Gorsky.

Left: Chakva. The Chinese tea specialist Lao Zhang Zhou with freshly planted tea on a plantation, 1905–15. Three-colour photograph by Sergei Prokudin-Gorsky. Both pictures are from the album *Views of the Caucasus and the Black Sea Region.*

Few were eager to take civilian posts, even very high ones, in the Caucasus, because it was an isolated region, ablaze with uprising, where the mountain passes were still held by hostile tribes, a region marked by frequent conflicts with the Turks. However, military men and others who liked to be where there was fighting were attracted to the Caucasus.

COUNT SERGEI WITTE, *The Memoirs*

Above: A couple from Dagestan, North Caucasian federal district, 1905–15. The man is in Cossack uniform and his wife is wearing traditional costume. Three-colour photograph by Sergei Prokudin-Gorsky, from the album *Views of the Caucasus and the Black Sea Region.*

Opposite below right: Kacheti in northeast Georgia. Grape harvest on the southern slopes of the Great Caucasus, *c.* 1890. Photograph by Dimitri Ermakov.

There a tattered Nogay labourer, with prominent cheekbones, brings a load of reeds from the steppes, turns his creaking cart…past a puddle that reaches nearly across the street….

LEO TOLSTOY, *The Cossacks*

Above: Armenia. Cart drawn by four horses, *c.* 1910. Photograph.

Left: Group of Armenians, *c.* 1900. Photograph.

Two huge eyes showed
A sorrow words cannot say....

OSIP MANDELSTAM, from *Stone*

Above: Armenian monk, 1859. Photograph from
Count Nostitz-Rieneck's expedition.

Right: Armenian woman with her children, seeking
refuge after the 1894–96 massacres in Turkey.
Photograph, 1899.

Above: Tbilisi, now capital of Georgia. View of the city from the path leading to Narikala Castle, *c.* 1890–1900. Photochrome.

Right: Tbilisi. Prince Lasarev's daughter in Tatar costume, *c.* 1890. Photograph by Dimitri Ermakov.

Opposite: Tbilisi. Carpet shop in Maidan, a suburb of the city, *c.* 1890–1900. Photograph by Dimitri Ermakov.

It was one of those wonderful evenings that occur only in the Caucasus. The sun had sunk...but it was still light. The evening glow had spread over a third of the sky.... The air was rarefied, motionless, and full of sound.

LEO TOLSTOY, *The Cossacks*

Above: Gagra, Abkhazia in Georgia. Sunset on the Black Sea, 1905–15. Three-colour photograph by Sergei Prokudin-Gorsky. Both pictures are from the album *Views of the Caucasus and the Black Sea Region*.

Opposite: Woman from Georgia in traditional costume, 1905–15. Three-colour photograph by Sergei Prokudin-Gorsky.

CENTRAL ASIA

Although Central Asian territories had been of interest to the Russian Empire since the days of Peter the Great, it was not until the later nineteenth century that they formally became part of it. Like those of the southwestern Empire, the native, non-Slavic inhabitants of Central Asia were officially registered as *inorodtsy* ('people of another origin'). They included the peoples of today's Turkmenistan and vast Kazakhstan, bordering the eastern Caspian Sea, Kyrgyzstan (Kirgizia), Uzbekistan and neighbouring Tajikistan (all at that time collectively known as Russian Turkestan). Apart from the Tajiks, who spoke a Persian tongue, the peoples of Central Asia were overwhelmingly speakers of Turkic languages and dialects. The predominant religion throughout the region was Sunni Islam, with Ismaili Shi'ites in the Pamir Mountains.

Central Asia was the heartland of the strategic rivalry between the Russian and British Empires, spanning the nineteenth century and beyond, which was known to the Russians as 'The Tournament of Shadows' and to the British as 'The Great Game'. The instability of the declining Ottoman Empire encouraged the two great powers in their battle for control over the enormous region, with Russia's perennial need for warm water ports counterbalanced by British determination to prevent Russian access to India, 'the jewel in the crown' of Britain's empire. The rivalry between the two powers led to the Crimean War of 1853–56 and in 1884 almost led to war again. Prime Minister Benjamin Disraeli wrote to Queen Victoria of his intention to 'clear Central Asia of Muscovites and drive them into the Caspian', and in 1878 he created the title of 'Empress of India' for the Queen, thereby raising her to the same international rank as the Russian Tsar.

Although the British gained much of Afghanistan, their buffer state protecting India, and Persia was parcelled out between the two powers, the Russians were the overall victors of the Great Game. The vast

territories they acquired included the Emirate of Bukhara and, in 1868, the legendary city of Samarkand, fourteenth-century seat of Tamerlane, last of the nomadic emperors, and since antiquity a principal point on the Great Silk Road to China. Like Bukhara to the west, Samarkand (in present-day Uzbekistan) is one of the oldest cities in the world, known as a 'large and splendid' place since the days of Marco Polo. Some years later, the Khanate of Khiva was also incorporated into the Russian Empire. Unlike Samarkand, Bukhara and Khiva remained as dependent protectorates with some internal autonomy.

In 1888, Samarkand became a terminus on the Trans-Caspian Railway, begun eleven years before. The Russians had originally intended the railway as a supply line for their armies fighting the local peoples opposed to Russian rule, but it was also to prove vital in the economic development of the region. Within five years of its construction, cotton exports from Central Asia had increased four-fold and imports of manufactured goods and building materials had provided an important impetus for further settlement and development.

By 1906, the Trans-Caspian Railway ran in a continuous line from Orenburg in European Russia to Tashkent (now in Uzbekistan), prompting an inflow of ethnic Russians to the Central Asian region. Competition for land and scarce water resources led to growing tensions. In 1916, the conscription of the previously exempt local peoples into the imperial army's labour battalions sparked a major revolt against the Russians. This Basmachi Revolt continued beyond the fall of the Empire in 1917 into an ongoing resistance to the new Soviet forces. During the Civil War, the fighting turned inwards too, with indigenous forces of mostly younger men supporting the Red Army against the traditional Central Asian rulers aided by White Russian and British forces.

Despite the short-lived Alash Autonomy in the Kazakh Steppes and the Kokand

Autonomy in present-day Uzbekistan, by the early 1920s, Russian
Central Asia had been absorbed into the new Soviet Union. A determined programme of Russification began, hand in hand with
intensive economic exploitation of the region.

Above: Ekhia, Bashkortostan, in the Volga federal district. Bashkiri man in front of his wooden house, 1910. The Bashkiri are a Turkic people living in the southern Ural Mountains. Three-colour photograph by Sergei Prokudin-Gorsky.

Left: Ekhia, Bashkortostan. Bashkiri woman in traditional costume, 1910. Three-colour photograph by Sergei Prokudin-Gorsky. Both pictures are from the album *Views of the Ural Mountains with Studies of the Industrial Region*.

Opposite: Woman, probably Turkoman or Kirgiz, in all her finery, standing in front of a Kazakh yurt, the traditional tent of the nomads in Central Asia, 1905–15. Three-colour photograph by Sergei Prokudin-Gorsky, from the album *Views of Central Asia*.

I was impressed by the vast, untapped resources of Central Asia,
which I was seeing for the first time [in 1890]. Although cotton
production has increased there in the intervening years
(to 1912), its resources are still largely untapped.

COUNT SERGEI WITTE, *The Memoirs*

Opposite and above: Mount Chapan-Ara with sixteenth-century mosque, near Samarkand in modern Uzbekistan, 1905–15. Three-colour photograph by Sergei Prokudin-Gorsky.

Right: Golodnaya Steppe, now in Uzbekistan. A Kirgiz nomad with his family, 1905–15. Three-colour photograph by Sergei Prokudin-Gorsky. Both pictures are from the album *Views of Central Asia*.

I had to take the letter...to the Bokharan consul.... I went to his house. A well-dressed Bokharan, in a large white turban, was sitting in the archway looking onto the street.... I approached him with my letter, on which [his] secretary pulled me rudely back, told me to stand back, take off my hat and wait while he presented my letter.... The Amir spoke French, having been in the Corps de Page, at the Tsar's court.

F. M. BAILEY, *Mission to Tashkent*

There is only one way of Russifying alien nationalities – have as many children as possible.

KOZNYSHEV, in Tolstoy's *Anna Karenina*

Above: Kirgiz tribal elders, Uzbekistan, *c.* 1900. Photograph.

Opposite: Russian settlers in the Mugan Steppe between the Talysh Mountains and the Caspian Sea, now in Azerbaijan, 1905–15. During the nineteenth century, it was official government policy to encourage ethnic Russians to settle in the border regions of the Russian Empire, such as South Caucasus. Three-colour photograph by Sergei Prokudin-Gorsky, from the album *Views of the Caucasus and the Region of the Black Sea.*

Left: Samarkand, now in Uzbekistan. Crowd in the Registan, 1911. This public square, with its three madrasas – Ulugh Beg (1417–20), Shir Dor (1619–36) and Tilla Kari (1646–60) – forms the heart of the old city. Three-colour photograph by Sergei Prokudin-Gorsky

We reached Samarkand before daylight.... The world-famous Registan, surrounded by magnificent mosques and colleges, looked neglected.... These unique beauties [were] erected when Tamerlane made this city his capital in the fourteenth city.

F. M. BAILEY, *Mission to Tashkent*

Above right: Samarkand. View from the Tilla Kari madrasa of the minaret and dome of the Shir Dor madrasa, 1911. Three-colour photograph by Sergei Prokudin-Gorsky.

Right: Samarkand, 1911. Mosaic on the wall of a tomb in the Shah-i Zinda necropolis. Three-colour photograph by Sergei Prokudin-Gorsky. All three pictures are from the album *Views of Central Asia*.

Left: Samarkand. Veiled Muslim woman in traditional dress covering the whole body, 1911. Three-colour photograph by Sergei Prokudin-Gorsky.

Below: Samarkand. Uzbek child in the courtyard of the Tilla Kari madrasa. Three-colour photograph by Sergei Prokudin-Gorsky.

She could not read but the list [of names] was read to her; she came back with the, to me, amazing statement that she did not know... her own surname!

F. M. BAILEY, *Mission to Tashkent*

Opposite: Samarkand, 1911. Group of Jewish children with their teacher. This oasis, which lay on the Silk Road, had grown since antiquity into a multi-ethnic community of Tajiks, Persians, Uzbeks, Russians, Arabs and Jews. Three-colour photograph by Sergei Prokudin-Gorsky. All three pictures are from the album *Views of Central Asia*.

This page and opposite: In the markets of Samarkand, 1911. Three-colour photographs by Sergei Prokudin-Gorsky, from the album *Views of Central Asia*.

Melon seller at his stall (opposite); dealer with colourful textiles and carpets of silk and wool (left); kebab restaurant (below and bottom right); tea room (bottom left).

In Samarkand I bought the best and largest grapes I had ever seen, nearly as large as walnuts. I also bought two round baskets of enormous raisins which were subsequently a great luxury on our desert journey.

F. M. BAILEY, *Mission to Tashkent*

THE FAR EAST

The Russian Far East extended from the shores of Lake Baikal in Siberia through Manchuria to the Pacific Ocean and beyond. It included the island of Sakhalin and even reached across the Bering Sea to Alaska.

Alaska had become part of the Empire long before the rest of the eastern territories, and it was also the first to leave. It formed by far the largest part of 'Russian America', which also included settlements in California and the Hawaiian islands. In the seventeenth century, Russian explorers had been the first Europeans to visit Alaska, and in 1742 it became an imperial colony. Fur trading settlements were established, but by the mid-nineteenth century, the resistance of the native people and the depletion of animal stocks through overhunting had decreased Russian interest in it, and in 1867 the territory was sold to the United States, along with the other American settlements, for two cents per acre.

Heavily forested Sakhalin, lying off the coast of Manchuria to the north of Japan, is Russia's largest island. Rival Japanese claims to it led to a series of treaties in the nineteenth century, allowing nationals of both powers to live there, and in 1857 a Russian katorga (penal colony) was established on the island. In 1890, the writer Anton Chekhov spent three months on Sakhalin conducting interviews for a census of the convicts, some of whose children had been transported with them, and also of the free settlers there. Chekhov described the penal colony as 'hellish', writing that he had witnessed there 'the extreme limits of human degradation'. By the turn of the twentieth century, Sakhalin's few thousand indigenous people (Ainu, Orok and the semi-nomadic Nivkh) were outnumbered by Russians, including some 22,000 convicts and about 10,000 settlers. Part of the settlers' work was to administer the prisons, but they also established coal mines and set up schools and churches for their own communities.

The Russians had signed a first border treaty with the Manchu Qing dynasty as early as 1689, and over the course of the nineteenth century, they gained extra territory from a China weakened by its Opium Wars with Britain. By the 1858 Treaty of Aigun, the Russians acquired all of Outer Manchuria, north of the Amur River, the border between the two empires, and in 1860 they gained not only Sakhalin but also Vladivostok on Golden Horn Bay, at the easternmost point of the Russian mainland. The Chinese had mined gold in the Vladivostok area, but for the Russians it was to prove more important as a free port and naval base and as a centre of shipbuilding. The extension of the Trans-Siberian Railway through to Vladivostok, its end station, was a vital impetus to its economic development, but the city's limitations were nonetheless to prove fatal to the empire.

Vladivostok was not an ice-free port; had it been so, the Russians would have had no need to lease the all-year port of Lüshun (formerly Port Arthur) from the Chinese, and the Russo–Japanese War, as Sergei Witte noted, might never have happened. Rival ambitions for influence in East Asia led to a surprise Japanese attack on Port Arthur in 1904; the ensuing nineteen months of fighting were to end in a humiliating Russian defeat, including the almost total annihilation of the imperial fleet at the Battle of Tsushima, viewed by historians as 'the greatest naval event since the Battle of Trafalgar'. The Russians had largely relied on their new Trans-Siberian Railway to transport troops, ammunition and supplies, but in 1904 it consisted of just a single line, so transports could take place in only one direction at a time: the resulting delays were a major factor in Russia's eventual defeat, and the defeat itself was a powerful impetus to the 1905 Revolution.

Vladivostok was also to be of great strategic importance for White and allied forces after the 1917 Revolution; the Red Army's capture of the city in October 1922 marked the end of the Civil War and the Bolsheviks' final victory.

Opposite: The Russian Empire. From *The Royal Illustrated Atlas of Modern Geography*, A. Fullarton & Co. Edinburgh, London and Dublin, 1872, pl. VI (detail).

Below: Vladivostok. Chapel, *c.* 1890. Photograph.

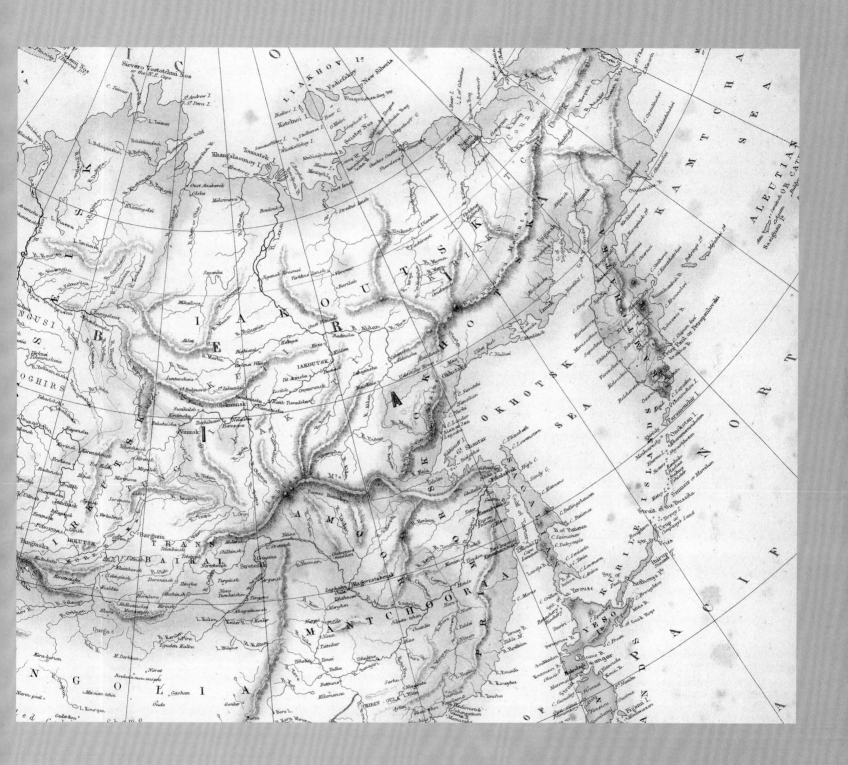

Left above: Vladivostok, in the Far Eastern federal district. Post office, c. 1910. Picture postcard

Left centre: Vladivostok. Packing department of the trading company Kunst & Albers, c. 1893. Photograph.

Left: Vladivostok. The station marking the terminus of the Trans-Siberian Railway, c. 1910. Picture postcard.

I stopped in Vladivostok. Of...our eastern coast in general with its fleets, problems, and dreams of the Pacific all I can say is: what crying poverty! The poverty, ignorance and pettiness are enough to drive you to despair. For every honest man there are ninety-nine thieves who are a disgrace to the Russian people.

ANTON CHEKHOV, Letters of 27 June and 9 December 1890

The prisoners, though wearing shackles, could walk freely
around the whole gaol; they swore, sang songs, did their
own work, smoked their pipes, and some (though a very few)
even drank liquor; and cards were played at night.

FYODOR DOSTOEVSKY, *Notes from the Dead House*

Opposite: Sakhalin, in the Far Eastern federal district, 1890. 'In Duiskaya Prison, the inmates are put in chains before they go to work.' From the nineteenth century onwards, the island was a penal colony for Russian convicts. Photograph by I. I. Pavlovski, from Anton Chekhov's private collection.

Right: Russians banished to Siberia, standing outside their barracks. Photograph by Keystone, *c.* 1910.

Below: George Kennan (1845–1924), the American explorer, wearing the typical clothes and chains of a Russian banished to Siberia, *c.* 1885–86. Photograph.

I spent three months plus two days on Sakhalin…. My work was strenuous; I took a complete and detailed census of the entire Sakhalin population and saw everything except an execution…. While I was living on Sakhalin, I felt nothing more than a certain bitterness in my innards, the sort that comes from rancid butter, but now, when I think back on it, Sakhalin seems to me like hell itself.

ANTON CHEKHOV, Letter of 9 December 1890

Opposite: Burjats, a Mongolian people, form the largest national minority in Siberia. Photograph, *c.* 1900.

Right: The Giljaks, a people indigenous to Siberia and the Far East, live mainly in the north of the island of Sakhalin. Picture postcard, 1905 (phototype Scherer, Nabholz & Co., Moscow).

Below: Siberian mail sled on a cold winter's morning, *c.* 1885–86. Photograph by George Kennan's travelling companion George A. Frost.

Right: The Russo–Japanese War, 1904–5. The Russian ships *Pallada* (left) and *Pobeda* (right) were destroyed below Fort Golden Hill in Port Arthur (the district of Lushunku in what is now the Chinese port of Dalian on the Yellow Sea). The war between the two empires began in February 1904, with the Japanese attack on Port Arthur, and after a series of heavy defeats for the Russians, it ended in autumn 1905. Stereo photograph, 1904, by Underwood & Underwood.

Painful and contradictory news has again arrived relating to the unhappy encounter at Tsushima. I received three reports. Alix and I went for a walk. The weather was superb and warm. We took tea and dined on the balcony.

TSAR NICHOLAS II, *Journal intime*

It was galling to represent a great military power that had acted stupidly and been defeated badly. But it was the infantile regime under which we had been living for some years past, not Russia, not the Russian army, that had been beaten.... Of course, they hated me for uttering the kind of truth that the Tsar seldom heard and never grew accustomed to hearing.

COUNT SERGEI WITTE, *The Memoirs*

Left: The Russo–Japanese War, 1904–5. Russian soldiers mourn their lost comrades in Port Arthur, which was then under siege, 1905. Stereo photograph by Underwood & Underwood.

With the nationwide consternation and resentment against the
government engendered by the destruction of the Russian fleet
by the Japanese at Tsushima, all those who opposed the regime,
from extremists to moderates, became united.

NICOLAS DE BASILY, *Memoirs*

Above: The corpses of Russian soldiers before their burial in Port Arthur, 1905.
Stereo photograph by Underwood & Underwood.

SIBERIA

The vast territory of Siberia encompasses much of the Eurasian Steppe, with its historic overland trade routes, and almost the whole of northern Asia, from the Ural Mountains in the west to the Pacific Ocean in the east, and from the Arctic in the north to Kazakhstan, Mongolia and China in the south. Parts of Siberia have belonged to Russia since the first victory of Ivan the Terrible's Cossacks over the Tatars in 1582. In the ensuing decades, the eastward movement of soldiers, explorers and fur traders undermined the power of the local khans and divided the loyalties of their vassal tribes. By 1639, the Russians had passed through Siberia to reach the Pacific, and in 1640 the entire territory became formally part of the Empire.

The diverse cultures of the indigenous peoples of Siberia survived into the Soviet period, as did their languages, some 120 in total. They included the Uralic languages, the Altaic family of Turkic, Mongolic and Tungusic languages, the Yeniseian languages of central Siberia and, apparently the oldest of all, a number of unrelated Palaeosiberian languages of the eastern regions. Many of these peoples were nomadic reindeer herders and hunters, while others were small farmers or gatherers of valuable nuts for trade. Some Altaic peoples mined iron ore and produced skilled metalwork.

By the end of the Empire, however, the indigenous peoples in most parts of Siberia had long been outnumbered by ethnic Russians. In the later nineteenth century, farming communities were established by religious dissidents refusing the authority of the Orthodox Church; they grew wheat, oats and potatoes – the last a crop not much favoured elsewhere in the Empire, since, as Alexander Herzen noted, 'Russian peasants were not very keen on planting potatoes, as though an instinct told them that this was a low-grade kind of food, which would give them neither health nor strength'. Fur trading continued, though over-trapping reduced its importance. During the summer, steam-powered ships and barges began to ply the Ob, the Yenisei and the Lena, the three great Siberian rivers. During the frozen winter months, horse-drawn sleds hauled goods and passengers over the same rivers, as well as over the territory's few roads. Towards the end of the nineteenth century, Siberia, like the rest of the Empire, underwent an enormous increase in industrialization, particularly in the mining of coal, lead and silver. Gold miners came too, though mostly to pan and dig alone. In 1891, work began on the great Trans-Siberian Railway. When completed in 1916, it ran from Moscow through southern Siberia to Vladivostok in the Far East.

Siberia's remoteness and harsh climate made it unattractive to all but the most determined settlers. After 1861, newly emancipated serfs were permitted to take up free land there, but conditions were primitive and few were anxious to do so. Writing from Tomsk in 1890 to his sister in the lively city of Moscow, Anton Chekhov notoriously remarked: 'Tomsk is a very dull town. To judge from the drunkards whose acquaintance I have made and from the intellectual people who have come to the hotel to pay their respects to me, the inhabitants are very dull too.'

It was the same remoteness that, in the eyes of the authorities, made Siberia an ideal place for exiles and convicts. Parts of the territory had been used as penal colonies from as early as 1590, but in the nineteenth century this practice increased dramatically. Political dissidents, including the writer Fyodor Dostoevsky, were transported by the hundreds of thousands, while serf owners and, later, community elders frequently shipped off their unwanted old or disabled, with the result

Opposite: The Russian Empire. From *The Royal Illustrated Atlas of Modern Geography*, A. Fullarton & Co. Edinburgh, London and Dublin, 1872, pl. VI (detail).

Below: Crevasse in the Altai Mountains, a massif in southern Siberia, c. 1910. Picture postcard.

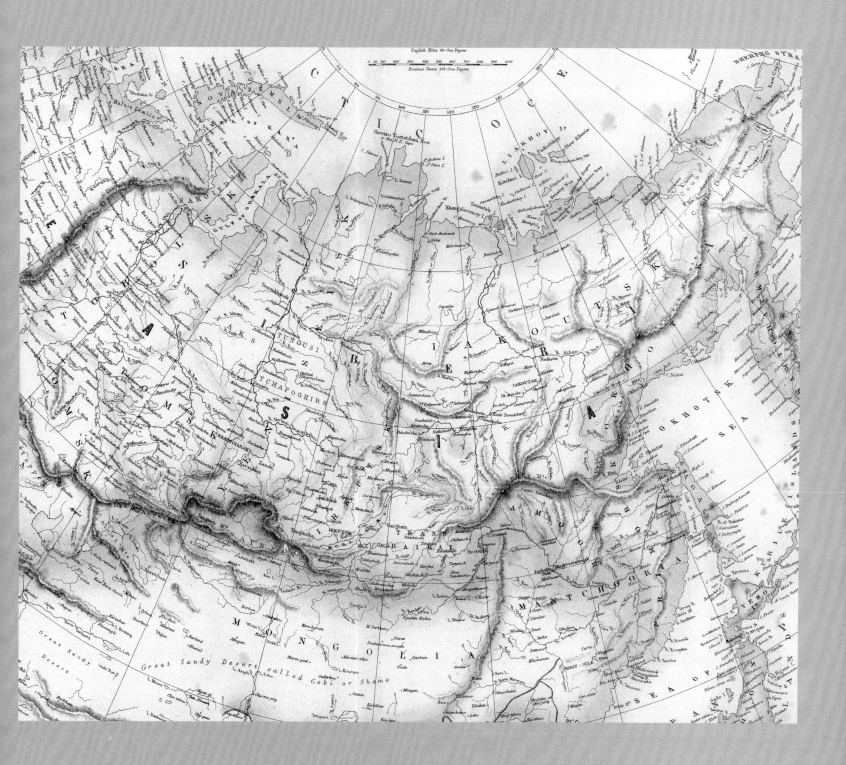

that Siberia became not only a prison but also a place of exile for the elderly.

The most famous of all Siberian prisoner-exiles were undoubtedly the last Tsar, Nicholas II, and his family. While the Provisional Government held, the Romanovs were kept under comfortable house arrest at the Governor's mansion in the old Siberian capital of Tobolsk, but on Kerensky's fall in October 1917, they were transferred to Yekaterinburg in the Urals.

After the Revolution, Siberia declared itself an autonomous republic. This was quickly overthrown by White forces, who established a capital in Omsk, but by early 1920 Siberia had fallen to the Bolsheviks.

The work itself did not seem too hard, and it was only much later that I realised that it was hard labour not because it was arduous and never-ending, but because it was forced....

FYODOR DOSTOEVSKY, *Notes from the Dead House*

I remember that each year, exactly like the one before, passed so slowly and so miserably. I remember that those long boring days were as monotonous as the sound of rainwater dripping from a roof, drop by drop. I remember that it was only my passionate longing for resurrection, rejuvenation and a new life that gave me the strength to wait and to hope.

FYODOR DOSTOEVSKY, *Notes from the Dead House*

Opposite: Siberia. Workers at one of the goldmines on the Lena, *c.* 1910. Photograph.

Right above: Tomsk, western Siberia. Panorama of the city, *c.* 1885–86. Photograph.

Right centre: Mooring place on the Mezhevaya Utka River, western Siberia. 1912. Three-colour photograph by Sergei Prokudin-Gorsky, from the album *Views of the Ural, of Western Siberia, and of the Waterways*.

Right: Mariinsk, central Siberia. Main street of the city, *c.* 1890. Photograph by Anton Chekhov.

Far left: A pointsman working for the Trans-Siberian Railway, 1910. Three-colour photograph by Sergei Prokudin-Gorsky, from the album *Views of the Ural Mountains with Studies of the Industrial Region*.

Left: Trans-Siberian Railway (Central Siberian stretch). Construction of the steel-truss bridge over the Yenisei, southwest of Krasnoyarsk, Siberia, 1893–96.

The Trans-Siberian Railway (1891–1906). The first sod was turned by the future Tsar Nicholas II in May 1891 just outside Vladivostok, while at the same time construction also began at Chelyabinsk on the Ural River. Because of the enormous distances involved (over 5,600 miles in all), construction of the railway was divided into different sections, some of which were begun at the same time. The individual administrative bodies (West Siberian, Central Siberian, Transbaikali, Amur and Ussuri Railways) were named after these different sections. By 1894, Omsk was already linked to the Ural, by 1895 to the Ob, and on 16 August 1898 the first train reached Irkutsk. Despite this progress, however, only the first half of the tracks had been laid by 1900. The railway was not completed until October 1916, with the opening of the Amur Bridge near Khabarovsk.

Above: Trans-Siberian Railway (West Siberian stretch). Bridge at the confluence of the Irtysh and the Om, near Omsk, *c.* 1900. Picture postcard (phototype Scherer, Nabholz & Co., Moscow).

Left: Trans-Siberian Railway (West Siberian stretch). Station in Ob near Novosibirsk, 1906. Picture postcard.

Above: West Siberia. Service in a railway carriage furnished as a mobile church and standing in a siding, c. 1890. Photograph by Anton Chekhov.

Right: Trans-Siberian Railway. The so-called Siberian Bridge across Lake Baikal. Until the opening of the railway all the way round the lake, vehicles, cargo and passengers had to be transported from the west bank to the east, near Mysovaya, by two ferryboats in the summer and by horse drawn sleds in the winter when the lake was frozen. Picture postcard, c. 1905.

Above: Siberia. Reindeer are an alternative form of transport in the tundra, *c.* 1900. Photograph.

Right: Sled drawn by three reindeer in the tundra, *c.* 1900. Photochrome.

Above: A Tuvan shaman at work, *c. 1900.* The Tuvans (along with the Soyots) form the largest non-Russian section of the population in the Altai–Sayan region of southern Siberia. Photograph.

Right: A group of Tungus, *c. 1900.* Manchu–Tungu is an all-embracing term for non-Russian ethnic minorities living in parts of Siberia, China and Mongolia. Photograph.

Opposite: Russian settlers in Siberia, *c. 1900.* Photograph.

Generally speaking, the Siberian race is healthy, well-grown,
intelligent, and extremely steady. The Siberian children of
settlers know nothing of the landowners' power. There is no
upper class in Siberia...; the officials and the officers, who are
the representatives of authority, are more like a hostile
garrison...than an aristocracy. The immense distances
save the peasants from frequent contact with them....

ALEXANDER HERZEN, *My Past and Thoughts*

Grey morning, later lovely and sunny. Baby [the Tsarevich] had a slight cold. In the morning we all went outside for half an hour. Olga and I sorted out our medicine. T[atiana] read to us from the Holy Bible.... Embroidered. The commandant comes into our room every day. Eight o'clock. Supper. [The young servant] Levka Sedniev was called out suddenly, he's allowed to go and see his uncle and he flew off – I'd like to know whether it's true, and whether we'll see the boy again!! Played bezique with N[icholas]. To bed at half past ten. 15 degrees.

TSARINA ALEXANDRA, Last diary entry, 3/16 July 1918. A few hours later, the Tsarina and Tsar Nicholas II, together with their five children and their attendants, were shot.

Right: Tsarskoye Selo, near St Petersburg, spring 1917. Tsar Nicholas II and his son Alexei, shovelling snow in the gardens of the castle where the family were kept under house arrest from March to August 1917, after the abdication. Photograph.

Below left: Tsarskoye Selo, spring 1917. Tsar Nicholas II (centre, with a shovel in his hand), and Grand Duchess Tatiana with a friend, gardening in the park. Photograph.

Below right: Tobolsk, Ural, 1917. The Tsar's family with entourage in front of the main entrance to the governor's residence during their internment from August 1917 to April 1918. Photograph by Underwood & Underwood.

THE URALS

The Ural Mountains serve as a northern boundary between the continents of Europe, to the west, and Asia, to the east. The mountain chain stretches more than 1,600 miles from the Arctic Ocean in the north to Kazakhstan in the south.

The Urals had been of interest to the Russian Empire since the seventeenth century, when the region's vast mineral wealth began to be discovered. Early in the eighteenth century, Peter the Great ordered a comprehensive geographical survey and the Russians began extracting valuable ores. The western Urals region has oil, gas and potassium salts; in the east there are nickel oxide, chromite and magnetite, bauxite, gold and platinum. Modest coal deposits exist all over the region, and the Urals earth is also rich in precious and semi-precious stones, including emeralds, amethysts and diamonds.

As the nineteenth century progressed, increasing Russian exploitation of the Urals posed a major threat to the indigenous peoples. Although the northern taiga, with its dense coniferous forests, was soon supporting a major timber industry, its Uralic- and Samoyedic-speaking peoples were largely able to maintain their traditional way of life, fishing, hunting and herding reindeer. However, extensive industrial development across the southern steppe forced the Turkic-speaking nomads there to abandon their traditional horse-breeding for agriculture, particularly wheat-growing. Ethnic Russians migrating to work on newly cultivated farmland, as well as in the mines and factories, quickly outnumbered the native inhabitants of the south. The American diplomat George Kennan observed that, as was common elsewhere in the Empire, the mine and factory owners themselves 'had a habit of living in or near the compounds of their plants'.

The region's many rivers include the Kama, a major tributary of the Volga, and the Ural itself, the third longest river in Europe. Until the later nineteenth century, the rivers served as the major transport arteries for local industries, since roads remained few and basic and, in bad weather, impassable. Barges and other vessels were hauled up the rivers by *burlaki* (boatmen), their Russian name deriving from a Tatar word meaning 'homeless'. Many were indeed homeless, wandering the area in search of seasonal work; the winters were times of particular hardship for them, since there was little work to be had once the rivers froze over.

The coming of the railways made it even harder for the boatmen to earn a living. The first railway across the Urals was built in the 1870s, fifteen years before the Trans-Siberian line. It linked Perm, the administrative capital, with the metallurgical centre of Yekaterinburg on the Iset River, which subsequently became an important railway hub and junction for the Trans-Siberian line. Both Perm and Yekaterinburg had been founded in the early eighteenth century by ministers of Peter the Great, looking to exploit the natural resources of the area. By 1860, Perm was a bustling industrial town of more than 20,000 people, living from paper mills, metallurgy and steamboat building. In 1871, the Empire's first phosphorus factory was opened there. The strategic commercial importance of the Urals region was widely acknowledged, and in 1916, supported by the pioneer radio physicist Alexander Popov and the legendary Russian chemist Dmitri Mendeleev, creator of the first version of the periodic table of elements, a branch of St Petersburg University was opened in Perm.

After the fall of the Provisional Government and the Bolshevik seizure of power in October 1917, the former imperial family were transferred from their house arrest in Tobolsk, Siberia, to Yekaterinburg. Here, on the night of 16/17 July 1918, the Tsar and Tsarina, together with their daughters Olga, Tatiana, Maria and Anastasia, the Tsarevich Alexei and the family's attendants, were executed.

On the outbreak of civil war in October 1917, the industrial towns of the Urals

Opposite: The Russian Empire. From *The Royal Illustrated Atlas of Modern Geography*, A. Fullarton & Co. Edinburgh, London and Dublin, 1872, pl. VI (detail).

Below: Miners washing the sand for gold, *c.* 1910. Photograph.

became prime targets for both White and Bolshevik forces. In 1918, the munitions factories of Perm were captured by the Whites, but the following year the city was retaken by the Red Army. After the Bolshevik victory in the Civil War, Yekaterinburg (renamed Sverdlovsk) became the administrative centre of the Urals region.

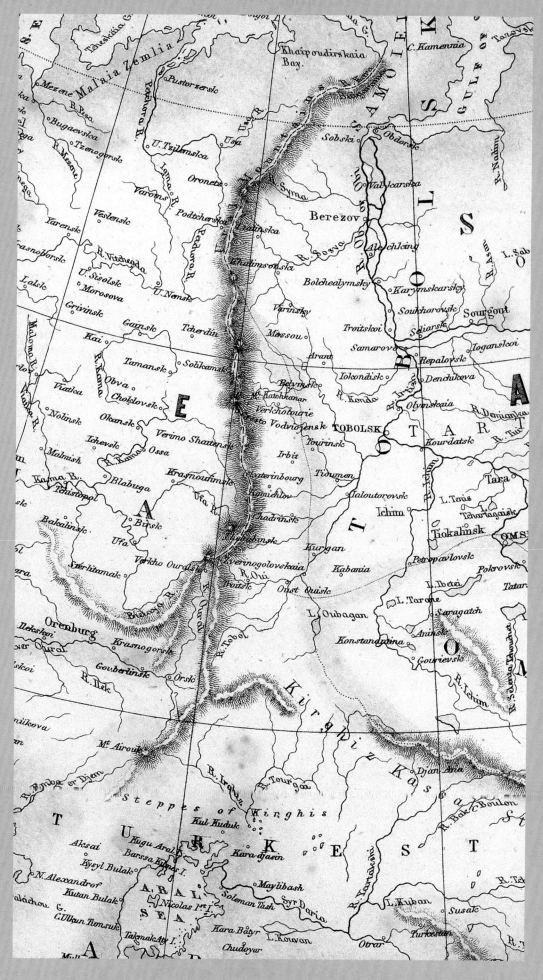

Above: Perm. The Old Siberian city gate, 1910. Three-colour photograph by Sergei Prokudin-Gorsky.

Left: Perm, in the Volga federal district. View of the western suburbs of this city on the Ural, seen from the railway bridge across the Kama River, 1910. Three-colour photograph by Sergei Prokudin-Gorsky.

Below: Perm, 1910. Metal girder bridge on stone piers across the Kama River, designed by Lev Proskuryakov for the Trans-Siberian Railway. Three-colour photograph by Sergei Prokudin-Gorsky. All three pictures are from the album *Views of the Ural Mountains with Studies of the Industrial Region*.

Workers? A working class? I know of no such class in Russia...
There are peasants, who constitute 90 percent of the
population. And among them is a comparatively small
number who work in mills and factories, but who,
nonetheless, remain peasants. [The socialists are] seeking
artificially to create some sort of new class, some sort of new
social relations, all completely alien to Russia.

KONSTANTIN POBEDONOSTSEV, Adviser to the last three Tsars

Above: Industrial region in Ural. Ironworks, c. 1910. Picture postcard.

Right: Industrial region in Ural. Test drilling, c. 1910. Picture postcard.

Opposite: Industrial region in Ural. Workers employed to transport wood to a smelting furnace for iron ore, 1910. Three-colour photograph by Sergei Prokudin-Gorsky, from the album *Views of the Ural Mountains with Studies of the Industrial Region*.

Opposite: Nizhny Tagil, Ural, 1910. Blast furnace for copper smelting in a smeltery built by the Brothers Demidov in 1720–25. The town in central Ural, near Yekaterinburg, is famous for its iron industry. Photograph by Sergei Prokudin-Gorsky.

Above: Satka, near Chelyabinsk, southern Ural. Blast furnace in the Troizko-Satkinski smeltery, 1910. Three-colour photograph by Sergei Prokudin-Gorsky. Both pictures are from the album *Views of the Ural Mountains with Studies of the Industrial Region*.

I do like life in general, but the kind of provincial,
parochial life we get in Russia – that I simply can't stand.

ASTROV, in Chekhov's *Uncle Vanya*

Opposite: A.P. Kalganov with son and granddaughter, 1910. Three generations of the family worked for the Zlatoust ironworks, founded in the mid-eighteenth century. Three-colour photograph by Sergei Prokudin-Gorsky.

Right: Zlatoust, 1910. View of the town in Central Ural which was founded in 1754 to set up an iron industry. Three-colour photograph by Sergei Prokudin-Gorsky.

Below: Zlatoust. Joinery in the Zlatoust sword blade factory, 1910. Three-colour photograph by Sergei Prokudin-Gorsky. All three pictures are from the album *Views of the Ural Mountains with Studies of the Industrial Region.*

I have cleaned up the house,
An obedient daughter,
And made up the soup
With the washing-up water.
I have swept up the dirt, the crumbs and the flies,
And baked all the sweepings into the pies.

Prison song, recorded by FYODOR DOSTOEVSKY
in *Notes from the Dead House*

Above: Women on a raft on the Tagil River – whose source is the eastern
slopes of the Ural Mountains near Yekaterinburg – preparing flax to
make linen, 1910. Three-colour photograph by Sergei Prokudin-Gorsky.
Both pictures from the album *Views of the Ural Mountains with Studies of
the Industrial Region*.

Right: Two Russian women farmers in traditional dress, *c.* 1900.
Picture postcard (phototype Scherer, Nabholz & Co., Moscow).

Opposite: Idyll on the Sim River in southern Ural, 1910. Three-colour
photograph by Sergei Prokudin-Gorsky.

Above: Fisherman on the Isset River, on the eastern slopes of the Ural Mountains, 1910. Three-colour photo by Sergei Prokudin-Gorsky.

Left: *Dacha* by a river in Ural, 1910. An idyllic setting for a typical Russian country house in which the owners would spend their weekends and summer holidays. Three-colour photograph by Sergei Prokudin-Gorsky.

Below: Shepherd boy on the Sim River in southern Ural, 1910. Three-colour photograph by Sergei Prokudin-Gorsky. All three pictures are from the album *Views of the Ural Mountains with Studies of the Industrial Region*.

Left: A cattle fence in Ural, 1910. Three-colour photograph by Sergei Prokudin-Gorsky.

Below: Farmer's wife spinning yarn outside her front door, 1910. Three-colour photograph by Sergei Prokudin-Gorsky, from the album *Views along the Upper Volga.*

Opposite: Artemiy, an early 'dropout', in front of his shack, where he practised his alternative lifestyle for more than forty years, 1910. Three-colour photograph by Sergei Prokudin-Gorsky, from the album *Views of the Ural Mountains with Studies of the Industrial Region.*

Above: Dalmatovo, near Kurgan, southern Ural, 1912. View from the bell-tower of the Uspenski Monastery, looking down on the town, which lies on the fringes of the west Siberian lowlands. Three-colour photograph by Sergei Prokudin-Gorsky, from the album *Views of the Ural Mountains and West Siberia*.

Right: Vetluga, near Nizhniy Novgorod, Volga. Church on the Vetluga River, a tributary of the Volga, 1910. Three-colour photograph by Sergei Prokudin-Gorsky, from the album *Views of the Ural Mountains with Studies of the Industrial Region*.

Right: Father Superior
Ksenofont, Abbot of the
Nicholas Monastery
in Verkhoturye, near
Sverdlovsk, on the eastern
edge of the Ural, 1910.
Photograph by Sergei
Prokudin-Gorsky.

Below: Monks planting
potatoes, 1910. Three-
colour photo by Sergei
Prokudin-Gorsky, from
the album *Views along the
Upper Volga*.

Opposite: The monk
Makariy outside his cell in
the Nicholas Monastery,
Verkhoturye, 1910. Three-
colour photograph by
Sergei Prokudin-Gorsky.
Both pictures are from the
album *Views of the Ural
Mountains with Studies of
the Industrial Region*.

Oh, you foot, you foot of the Church,
Oh, you light of the altar,
Our little father,
Hail to thee...!

Old Russian church song

You cannot imagine the deplorable material and moral
condition of our lower clergy. The sviatchenik of our rural
parishes almost always lives in a black misery where he loses all
sense of dignity, all decency, all respect for his clerical dress and
his function. The peasants despise him for his laziness and
drunkenness, and, what's more, he's always squabbling with
them over the price of the offices and sacraments. They don't
hesitate to harm him; they'll even give him a good thrashing....
Our socialists have been very clever in exploiting this pitiful
situation, especially among the young priests....

COUNT VLADIMIR NIKOLAEVICH KOKOVTSOV,
former prime minister, 29 March 1916

My house is there where the floor is the earth, the ceiling

the heavens, but the house has no walls and no roof....

Those that God has cursed live in this house....

OSIP, in Chekhov's *Platonov*

Above: Migrant day labourers
having a rest, *c.* 1900. Photograph.

Opposite: Homeless migrant farm labourer, *c.* 1900.
Picture postcard (phototype Scherer, Nabholz & Co., Moscow).

Above: Boatmen on a tributary of the Volga, *c.* 1895.
Photograph.

Opposite: Volga boatmen (*burlaki*), *c.* 1900. They were
employed on the Volga, long after the arrival of the first
steamships, to haul barges upstream. In Ilya Repin's most
famous painting (1873), they embody the suffering and
stoicism of the Russian people. Picture postcard.

MOSCOW & ENVIRONS

The city of Moscow takes its name from the Moskva River on whose banks it is built. Its location at the headwaters of the Volga was a major factor in its rapid rise to prominence and power, and from the medieval Grand Duchy of Muscovy, through the Tsardom established by Ivan the Terrible in 1547, to the foundation of St Petersburg in 1703, Moscow served as Russia's capital.

The mighty citadel of the Kremlin began as a simple wooden wall erected in the twelfth century to protect the emerging town. Italian masters added towers and churches in the late fifteenth century, and by the middle of the nineteenth century, the armoury and the Grand Kremlin Palace stood powerful witness to a seemingly unassailable autocracy.

To the northeast of Moscow, in the region once known as Zalesye, lie the famous 'Golden Ring' cities, with their kremlin fortresses, monasteries and beautiful onion dome churches. The original eight cities in the days of the Empire (others have been added since) are Sergiyev Posad, Pereslavl-Zalesski, Rostov Veliki, Yaroslavl, Kostroma, Ivanovo, Suzdal and Vladimir. Together they present a magnificent display of Russian architecture from the twelfth to the eighteenth centuries. The old Zalesye region was the heart of the medieval state of Vladimir-Suzdal, later the Grand Duchy of Moscow. Over the centuries, this region proved central to the development of the Russian state and the Empire, as well as to the power of the Orthodox Church.

In 1817, the centuries-old Makaryev Fair, drawing merchants from throughout European Russia and Central Asia and even from India, was transferred to Nizhny Novgorod, east of Moscow. This famous fair served as an entrepôt for almost half of all Russian exports, and by mid-century it had turned Nizhny into the trade capital of the Empire. A temporary bridge for the fair was built over the Oka River mouth to the great Volga and new railway links to Moscow in the later nineteenth century increased the pace of the city's economic development, so that by the turn of the twentieth century it was not only a vital commercial hub but a prime industrial centre as well, particularly for ironworks.

Nizhny Novgorod was the birthplace (in 1868) of the writer Maxim Gorky, a central figure in the literary life of Moscow and later in its political life too. Gorky's artistic circle included his close friend the playwright Anton Chekhov and Russia's most famous living novelist, Leo Tolstoy. Gorky often visited Tolstoy at his estate of Yasnaya Polyana to the south of Moscow, recording many of the great man's less literary utterances in a collection of lively reminiscences.

Chekhov's innovative plays were a mainstay of the new Moscow Arts Theatre, formed in 1898 by director Vladimir Nemirovich-Danchenko and actor–producer Constantin Stanislavski, founder of the influential school of 'method acting'. The theatre was a venue for naturalistic plays, which stood in powerful and very modern contrast to the melodramatic theatre then current in Moscow. Lenin's personal interest in the theatre ensured its survival for some years after the Revolution, though it eventually succumbed to the repressive artistic policies of the Bolshevik state.

It was not until the turn of the century that Moscow's Bolshoi Ballet began to achieve the fame it enjoys today. Though founded in the 1770s, it was long overshadowed by the imperial ballet of St Petersburg, until the appointment of choreographer Alexander Gorsky as ballet master in 1900. Like Stanislavski in the theatre, who inspired him, Gorsky favoured modern, naturalistic forms, as opposed to what he saw as the stilted academic dance of St Petersburg. Audiences at the Bolshoi also benefited from the extraordinary development of Russian music in the later nineteenth century, hearing regular performances of operas by Mussorgsky, Borodin and Tchaikovsky, among many others.

Though arguably first among Russian cities for its avant-garde artistic reputation, Moscow formally remained a provincial capital until after the Revolution. In March 1918, fearing an

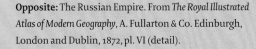

Opposite: The Russian Empire. From *The Royal Illustrated Atlas of Modern Geography*, A. Fullarton & Co. Edinburgh, London and Dublin, 1872, pl. VI (detail).

Below: Nizhny Novgorod. Rural bazaar, with tea being served, *c.* 1900. Photograph.

attack on Petrograd despite his peace treaty with Germany and the Central Powers, Lenin reluctantly withdrew his Bolshevik government to the Kremlin. Moscow, Lenin's 'foul city' of tsarist nostalgia, Orthodox religion and backward-looking peasant habits, became capital of the Russian Socialist Republic and, less than five years later, of the newly formed Union of Soviet Socialist Republics.

Opposite: Rostov Veliki ('Great Rostov'), one of the oldest cities in Russia, along with Suzdal, Uglich, Yaroslavl and Vladimir, part of the 'Golden Ring' around Moscow. The Resurrection Church in the Kremlin, 1911. Three-colour photograph by Sergei Prokudin-Gorsky, from the album *Views along the Upper Volga between Yaroslavl, Vladimir and Kostroma.*

Right: Ostashkov, near Tver, central Russia. View of the cemetery of the Church of the Exaltation of the Cross, 1910. Three-colour photograph by Sergei Prokudin-Gorsky, from the album *Views along the Upper Volga.*

When the soul takes its farewell,
over the pale body it sighs a lament:
Farewell, my pale body,
in the cold damp grave will you be buried,
and soon there'll be little over
from what the worms have left.

Old Russian church song

Are the Russians as religious as they're generally thought to be?
I often ask myself this question.... The people are more
religious, or at least more Christian, than the Church is. There is
more spirituality, more mysticism, more genuine feeling in the
piety of the masses than in any orthodox theology or dogma.
The official Church has become an instrument of autocracy,
a mixture of bureaucracy and police; day by day it loses
more of its sway over Russian souls.

MAURICE PALÉOLOGUE

Opposite: Kostroma, central Russia. The Epiphany Cathedral (1559–65) is the oldest building in the city, 1910. Three-colour photograph by Sergei Prokudin-Gorsky, from the album *Views along the Upper Volga between Kashin and Makarov.*

Above: Rostov Veliki, central Russia. Museum in the Prince's Palace, 1911. Three-colour photograph by Sergei Prokudin-Gorsky.

Left: Vladimir, central Russia. The Demetrius Cathedral, 1911. Three-colour photograph by Sergei Prokudin-Gorsky, from the album *Views along the Upper Volga between Yaroslavl, Vladimir and Kostroma.*

Above: Nizhny Novgorod, Volga. View of the city from the fortifications of the citadel, *c.* 1890–1900. Photochrome.

Left: Nizhny Novgorod. Panorama of the city, *c.* 1880. Photograph.

Below: Nizhny Novgorod. The Fair Bridge (now the Kanavinski Bridge) over the Oka, before it flows into the Volga, *c.* 1890–1900. Photochrome.

Left: Shoemaker's apprentice, 1900. Photograph by Natalya Nordman.

Below: Farmer from the Simbirsk region on the Volga, *c.* 1910. Photograph by William Carrick.

Opposite: Prosperous farmers from the areas around Nizhny Novgorod, *c.* 1880. Photograph.

I had heard that the merchants in the shopping arcades had received a stock of raw sheepskin jackets for adults and children from the Nizhny Novgorod fair, and I happened to mention this to my husband. He was very interested, mentioned that he himself used to wear a raw sheepskin jacket at one time, and wanted to buy one just like it for our Fedya…. We were shown a dozen or so jackets…Dressed in his…cap and sheepskin jacket…our plump, rosy little fellow was really handsome.

ANNA DOSTOEVSKY, *Dostoevsky: Reminiscences*

Come to Moscow!!! I've fallen terribly in love with Moscow. Once you've grown accustomed to Moscow, you'll never leave it again. I'm a Muscovite now, for good.

CHEKHOV, Letter to Kramaryov, 8 May 1881

Above: Moscow. View of the city from the Kremlin, *c.* 1910. Photograph.

Left: Moscow. The Bolshoy Kamenny Bridge or 'Great Stone Bridge' across the Moskva River, *c.* 1860. Built between 1687 and 1692, under the direction of Patriarch Filaret of the Russian Orthodox Church, it was known as the 'Eighth Wonder of the World'. Thieves and robbers often sought refuge beneath its arches. During the second half of the nineteenth century, it was replaced by an iron bridge, but retained its original name. Photograph.

Left: Moscow. Chapel of Our Lady of Iberia, near the Resurrection Gate of the Kremlin, *c.* 1890. Photograph.

Below: Moscow. Church procession, *c.* 1900. Photograph.

Opposite: Moscow. St Basil's Cathedral in the Kremlin, *c.* 1890. Photograph.

The minority feel the need of God because they have got everything else, the majority because they have nothing.

LEO TOLSTOY

Above: Moscow. Tsar Nicholas II and the Tsarina with their entourage entering the Kremlin to celebrate the 300th anniversary of the House of Romanov, 1913. Photograph.

Above: Moscow. The Tsar Bell in the Kremlin, 1900. The bell, cast in 1735 and one of the biggest in the world, was never rung, and since 1836 it has simply been one of the sights to see in the Kremlin. Photograph by Murray Howe.

Left: Moscow, 1909. The Tsar Cannon in the Kremlin, made in 1586, is the biggest cannon in the world, though it never fired a shot. Photograph by Murray Howe.

One evening at my house, very gently and without accompaniment [Feodor Chaliapin] began to sing. He was a giant, simple in manner and a bit unpolished, but richly gifted, as men of humble Russian origin often are.

NICOLAS DE BASILY, *Memoirs*

Above: Konstantin Stanislavski (1863–1938) was one the foremost actors and directors of his time and had a great influence on world theatre. Here we see him as an amateur, playing Don Juan in a performance of Alexander Pushkin's *The Stone Guest*, by the Moscow Society of the Arts, 1889. Photograph.

Left: Feodor Chaliapin (1873–1938), probably the most famous bass during the first half of the twentieth century, here appearing as the eponymous hero of Modest Mussorgsky's opera *Boris Godunov*, 1913. Photograph.

Above: Moscow, 1909. The Bolshoi Theatre, founded in 1776 and rebuilt in 1825 in neoclassical style after a fire. Photograph by Murray Howe.

Left: Feodor Chaliapin, at the height of his fame, posing for Ilya Repin in the latter's country house, 'Penaty', in Karelia, 1915. Photograph by Carl Bulla.

All is still in Moscow. Only quite rarely is the sound heard, here
and there, of wagon wheels crackling along the wintry street.

LEO TOLSTOY, *The Cossacks*

The Petrovka seemed a corner of Petersburg mislaid in Moscow. The matching houses…the quiet ornaments of the facades…the good tobacconist, the good restaurant with its…gas lamps…all helped to create the impression.

BORIS PASTERNAK, *Doctor Zhivago*

The restaurant itself was a blaze of light and colour. The long, high room was surrounded by a balcony on all sides. Along the balcony were gaily lit windows and doors opening into the private rooms – known in Russia as 'kabinets' – where, hidden from prying eyes, dissolute youth and debauched old age trafficked roubles and champagne for gypsy songs and gypsy love.

R. H. BRUCE LOCKHART, *Memoirs of a British Agent*

Above: Moscow. Interior of the Gryasi restaurant, *c.* 1900. Picture postcard.

Opposite left above: Moscow. Interior of the Yeliseyev Brothers' delicatessen in Tverskaya Street, 1901. Photograph.

Opposite left below: Moscow. Textile market near Red Square after closing time, 1886.

Opposite right: Typical uniform of a Moscow waiter, *c.* 1900. Picture postcard.

I still remember very well my first impressions of Moscow in 1876. I was just thirteen. After quiet, provincial Taganrog…Moscow really astounded me. Huge houses, wonderful theatres, endless streets, alleys, culs-de-sac that I was always losing myself in, countless businesses, shops, warehouses, noisy markets that reminded me of fairgrounds, the sound of the famous Moscow church bells, the horse-drawn trams rolling along on the rails – all of it really stimulated my imagination.

MARIA CHEKHOVA, *My Brother Anton Chekhov*

Above: Moscow. Sunday at the market around the Sukharev Tower, *c.* 1910. Photograph.

Below: Moscow. Russian women selling their textiles in an open-air market, 1909. Photograph by Murray Howe.

Right: Moscow. Market women and their customers, 1909. Photograph by Murray Howe.

The Okhotny Ryad (Hunters' Market) is the stomach of Moscow. Its name harks back to the days when it was still permitted to sell game here that hunters from outside the city had brought in.

VLADIMIR GILYAROVSKY, *Moscow and the Muscovites*

The market women came…to the flea market with their husbands and tenants and immediately stocked up with fresh goods bought directly, which they then sold straight away to other customers.

VLADIMIR GILYAROVSKY, *Moscow and the Muscovites*

Left: Moscow. Young street vendors, 1909. Photograph by Murray Howe.

Above: Moscow. The market around the Sukharev Tower, *c.* 1900. Photograph.

Right: Moscow. Street vendor selling cucumbers, 1909. Photograph by Murray Howe.

Left: Moscow. Woman selling headscarves, *c.* 1900. Photograph.

Right: Moscow. Women farmers bringing their wares to market, *c.* 1870. Photograph.

Below: Moscow. Peddler selling toys and sieves, *c.* 1900. Photograph.

The houses around Khitrov Market (Khitrovka) were divided
into residences that had one large or two or three smaller
rooms, sometimes with two-tier day beds, in which homeless
people, irrespective of age or sex, would spend the night....
Each tenant had his own clientele. Burglars lived with one,
vagabonds with another, thieves with the next, and at yet
another place there were simply poor people. Wherever there
are poor people, inevitably there are also children – future lags.
Anyone who is born in Khitrovka and manages to grow up in
this dreadful area ends up in prison. There are few exceptions.

VLADIMIR GILYAROVSKY, *Moscow and the Muscovites*

Two- and three-storey houses around the edges of the squares were full of people seeking refuge for the night, accommodating up to ten thousand souls. These houses brought their owners huge profit. Each overnight lodger paid a fiver for the night, whereas the single rooms were let for twenty.

VLADIMIR GILYAROVSKY,
Moscow and the Muscovites

Opposite: Moscow. Khitrovka Market. In this large square in the centre of the city, people sold anything and everything, even worn-out shoes, c. 1895. Photograph.

Right: Moscow. People living in a night shelter in Khitrovka Market, c. 1895. All around the square were two- and three-storey houses with night shelters to accommodate the poorest of the poor. Photograph.

A melancholy lull hung over the streets and it seemed that the pitiful buildings...hinting at the impoverished and boring life lurking within their walls, had originated for nothing. People appeared from time to time and even they were walking slowly as though without motivation, as though they could hardly overcome their somnolence....

FYODOR SOLOGUB, *The Petty Demon*

Above: Moscow. Two occupants of a night shelter, drunk on vodka, c. 1901. Photograph.

Opposite above left: Portrait of a boy in an apron, c. 1860. Photograph.

Opposite above centre: Young street vendors, c. 1900. Photograph by William Carrick.

Opposite above right: Portrait of an old woman, c. 1860. Photograph.

Opposite below: Moscow. View of Alexandrov Street, one of the arterial roads of the city, 1914. Photograph.

Above: Moscow. Demonstrations at the funeral of the revolutionary Nikolai Bauman, 20 October 1905. Photograph.

Right: Moscow. The city police search a suspicious passer-by, 1905. Photograph.

Opposite: Moscow. Street barricades during the first Russian Revolution, 1905. Photograph.

I won't say I wasn't affected by our [1905] revolution. Of course
I was. But I couldn't stand the compulsory requirement to fall
into ecstasies over it and to be indignant with the government…

VALERY BRYUSOV, *The Diary*

At all the stations soldiers were gathered in little knots of
six and seven; talking, arguing, gesticulating. Once a big,
bewhiskered mujik thrust his head in at a car window,
pointed menacingly at a well-dressed passenger and
bellowed interrogatively, 'Burzhouee!' (Bourgeois!).
He looked very comical, yet no one laughed.…

LOUISE BRYANT, *Six Red Months in Russia*

Left: Anton Chekhov with family and friends in the courtyard of his house at 6 Sadovo-Kudrinskaya Street in Moscow, *c.* 1890. Photograph. Anton Chekhov (1860–1904) studied medicine but pursued his medical career for only a short time before devoting himself to literature in the early 1880s. In 1890, he visited one of the notorious penal colonies on the island of Sakhalin. In 1901, he married Olga Knipper, an actress at the Moscow Arts Theatre. From 1887, he began to write plays, the most famous of which are *The Seagull* (1898), *Three Sisters* (1901), and *The Cherry Orchard* (1904), all of which are still produced worldwide.

Opposite left: Tolstoy in the year of his death, 1910. Photograph. Leo Tolstoy (1828–1910) was the son of a land-owning count and was educated at Kazan University. In 1853–56, he served as an officer in the Caucasian army during the Crimean War. From 1857 onwards, he lived alternately on the family estate of Yasnaya Polyana and in Moscow. Tolstoy began his literary career in 1852. Apart from *Anna Karenina* (or *Anna Karenin*; 1878), his novel about marriage, his masterpiece is the epic historical and philosophical novel *War and Peace* (1868–69). Tolstoy had considerable influence on the realist and naturalist literature that followed.

Chekhov had fine eyes. When he smiled they became warm and caressing, like a woman's. And his laughter, almost soundless, was somehow particularly fine. Laughing, he was enjoying the laughter, rejoicing. I don't know anyone else who could laugh so – if one can put it that way – 'spiritually'.

MAXIM GORKY, *Gorky's Tolstoy and other Reminiscences*

Every word of Goethe's got written down, but Tolstoy's thoughts are lost in the air. That, my friend, is intolerably Russian. Afterwards people will come to their senses and start writing memoirs, and they'll be full of lies.

ANTON CHEKHOV, in *Gorky's Tolstoy and other Reminiscences*

Right: Maxim Gorky in his black shirt, 1906. Photograph. In his youth, Maxim Gorky (1868–1936), who grew up without any formal education, wandered through large areas of Russia earning his living as a casual labourer. In 1892, he began to write, and in 1898, he became well known for his stories about tramps and other down-and-outs. In 1905, he met Lenin. He was a champion of proletarian literature and was one of the founders of socialist realism. Apart from his autobiographical writings, his most famous work is his play *The Lower Depths*, in which he vividly depicts the suffering of the poor.

Chekhov said, 'I said to [Tolstoy], Gorky is a good man. But he says: No, no. I know what I'm talking about. He has a duck's bill for a nose; the only people who have noses like that are the unhappy and the angry. Besides, women don't like him, and women can smell out a good man the way dogs can.' As he told me this he laughed until the tears came.

From MAXIM GORKY, *Gorky's Tolstoy and other Reminiscences*

Lingering there at a distance was an idle sweating stalwart with a coachman's beard, a blue jacket, and blacked boots. He was knocking back glass after glass. Now and then the idle sweating stalwart would summon the waiter.

'How's about a little somethin'?'

'Some melon, sir?'

'Your melon, it tastes like soap with sugar on it.'

'Perhaps a banana, sir?'

'That's a dirty-sounding fruit.'

ANDREI BELY, *Petersburg*

Left: Russian coachman in typical uniform, *c.* 1895. Photograph.

Opposite above: Moscow. Lyubyanskaya Square, 1902. The arched Vladimir Gate leads to the district of Kitay-gorod (meaning 'Chinatown'), which by the sixteenth century was already the most important trade centre in Moscow, bordering on the Kremlin and encompassing Red Square. Photograph by Otto Kirchner.

Opposite below: Russian coach with one horse, *c.* 1900. Picture postcard.

The day of the races was a very busy one for Karenin; but...he decided he would go to see his wife...and from there to the races, at which the whole Court was to appear.... He was going to see his wife because he was determined to keep up appearances.

LEO TOLSTOY, *Anna Karenina*

Above: Moscow. Grandstands at the Imperial Hippodrome, c. 1900. Photograph.

Left: Moscow. A box in the stand of the Imperial Trotting Association, 1909. Photograph by Murray Howe.

Above: Moscow. Grandstand at the Imperial Hippodrome, 1909. Photograph by Murray Howe.

And the battle has no end!
We only dream of peace
through the blood and dust...
And there is no end...
The frightened clouds
draw ever nearer
The sunset is bathed in blood.
Blood streams from the heart.
Weep, heart, weep.
There is no peace....

ALEXANDR BLOK, from
On the Field of Kulikovo

Above: The Russian army on manoeuvres. Infantrymen in a trench, *c.* 1910. Picture postcard.

Left: First World War. Dead Russian soldiers on the battlefield near Baranavich (White Russia), June 1916. Photograph.

Opposite: First World War. Dead soldier on the Eastern Front, *c.* 1916. Photograph.

Horrible rumours of Russians manning the trenches with nothing but sticks in their hands percolated through from the front to the countryside. Neither the old men nor the young recruits had any stomach for this slaughter....

R. H. BRUCE LOCKHART, *Memoirs of a British Agent*

Then for the Bolsheviki, Trotsky mounted the tribune, borne on a wave of roaring applause that burst into cheers and a rising house, thunderous. His thin, pointed face was positively Mephistophelian in its expression of malicious irony.

JOHN REED, *Ten Days That Shook the World*

Above: February Revolution 1917 in Moscow. A young man distributing leaflets, February 1917.

Left: October Revolution 1917 in Moscow. Leon Trotsky at a political meeting in Red Square, c. 1917–18. Photograph.

I am in despair that there is no news.... And I am in even greater despair about the fact that I have no means of getting my money out of the bank.... I have begun to develop a strong suspicion that my 2,000 roubles are going to be engulfed in the ocean of the Russian Revolution.

MIKHAIL BULGAKOV, Letter of 31 December 1917 to his sister Nadezhda

THE PHOTOGRAPHERS

Leonid Andreyev (1871–1919), dramatist and fiction writer. Born to a middle-class family in Oryol province southwest of Moscow, he studied law in Moscow and St Petersburg before beginning work as a police court reporter. Encouraged by Maxim Gorky to devote himself to fiction, Andreyev quickly became a literary superstar. An active supporter of democratic reform in the earlier years of the century, he was dismayed by the Bolshevik coup of 1917. Falling out of literary favour and hostile to the new regime, he withdrew to an impoverished life in Kuokkala, Finland, where he died of heart failure.

Carl Bulla (1853/55–1929), German–Russian photographer and pioneer of photojournalism. Born in the Prussian town of Leobschütz (now Głubczyce in Poland), Bulla ran away from home at the age of 10 or 12 to seek his fortune in St Petersburg. There he began working as a delivery boy for a photographic supplies shop, which led to more technical work making glass negative plates by hand; at 20 he opened a successful small factory to produce the same plates industrially. In 1875, Bulla opened a photographic portrait studio in St Petersburg, and became a naturalized Russian. Ten years later, on receipt of a police permit allowing him to photograph more widely, he began his photojournalistic work of street scenes and everyday life. In 1916, he retired to Ösel Island (now Saaremaa in Estonia), where he continued his own work and established classes to pass his technical knowledge on to aspiring photographers.

Roger Fenton (1819–69), English photographer best known for his images of the Crimean War (1853–56). Born into a wealthy Lancashire family, Fenton took a degree in classics and mathematics at the liberally oriented University College London before training privately as a painter. Inspired by the photographs displayed at the Great Exhibition of 1851 in London, he travelled to Paris to learn about waxed paper calotype (talbotype) techniques. Following a photographic journey in Russia, he returned to London to found the Photographic Society (later Royal Photographic Society) under the patronage of Prince Albert, the Prince Consort, at whose suggestion he was to travel to the Crimea in 1855 as Britain's first official war photographer. In 1862, Fenton sold his photographic equipment and gave up photography altogether.

Murray Howe (1869–1941), American sports journalist and photographer. Born in New Jersey, he began writing for *The Horse Review* in his twenties, eventually becoming secretary of Billings Park, a race track in Memphis, Tennessee, owned by C. K. G. Billings, founder of the petrochemicals pioneer Union Carbide. In 1909, Billings took his horses on an exhibition tour of Europe, including Russia, with Howe as the accompanying photojournalist. Soon after his return to America, Howe was appointed director of advertising for Union Carbide. A lively and popular figure, he was inducted into the Harness Racing Hall of Fame for his contributions to racing journalism.

William Carrick (1827–78), Scottish–Russian photographer. Born in Edinburgh, he was brought as an infant to Kronstadt in the Gulf of Finland, where his father worked as a timber merchant. He studied architecture in St Petersburg and Rome before deciding to become a photographer. In Edinburgh he met the photographic technician John MacGregor, with whom he subsequently set up a photography studio in St Petersburg. Carrick was a pioneer of ethnographic photography; patronized by members of the nobility, he also made a great many photographic prints of contemporary paintings. He died of pneumonia in St Petersburg.

George Kennan (1845–1924), American explorer and war correspondent, writer and lecturer. Born in Ohio, he began working in a telegraph office at the age of 12. The first of his three lengthy Russian journeys began with an 1864 contract to survey a proposed overland telegraph route through Siberia and across the Bering Strait to Kamchatka. He subsequently explored little-known areas of the Caucasus, also travelling in European Russia and western Siberia. Initially supportive of the autocratic Tsarist regime, which encouraged his journeys, he gradually became a determined opponent of it, lecturing for over 20 years on the necessity for revolution in Russia. He was nonetheless fiercely critical of the 1917 coup, regarding the Bolsheviks as self-serving and also incapable of resolving the country's enormous difficulties. The ethnographical content of Kennan's books has ensured their continuing validity.

Sergei Prokudin-Gorsky (1863–1944), pioneer of colour photography. Born in Vladimir province to a noble family, he studied chemistry, painting and music in St Petersburg before training in photochemistry and three-colour photography with Adolf Miethe in Berlin; this formed the basis of Prokudin-Gorsky's own later technique. In 1890, Prokudin-Gorsky married Anna Lavrova, daughter of the Russian industrialist Aleksandr Lavrov, becoming director of the executive board of Lavrov's metal works near St Petersburg, a position he retained until the October revolution of 1917. In 1901, he established a photographic studio and laboratory in St Petersburg, later becoming editor of *Fotograf-Liubitel*, Russia's principal photography journal. Prokudin-Gorsky's own work was widely praised, and in 1909 he was commissioned by Tsar Nicholas II to undertake a documentary journey through the Empire, during which he produced some 10,000 colour photographs of landscapes and peoples. Though offered a professorship under the Bolshevik regime, Prokudin-Gorsky left Russia in 1918 for Paris, where he lived to the end of his life,

THE WRITERS

Anna Akhmatova (1889–1966), *nom de plume* of Anna Andreyevna Gorenko, poet and translator. Born in the village of Bolshoy Fontan near Odessa, she grew up in comfortable circumstances in Tsarskoye Selo near St Petersburg. She achieved an early success with her intimate and colloquial style of poetry, becoming a founder of the Acmeist school, which emphasized craft and conciseness over the mysticism of the rival Symbolist school. Under Stalinism, Akhmatova's work was suppressed, circulating only in *samizdat*. Two of her husbands were executed by the regime, and her son Lev spent many years in the Gulag. After Stalin's death, Akhmatova was gradually rehabilitated; her masterpiece *A Poem without a Hero* was finally published in the Soviet Union during the *perestroika* period of the late 1980s, and today she is considered among the finest poets of the twentieth century. Akhmatova died of heart failure in Moscow and is buried in St Petersburg.

Frederick Marshman Bailey (1882–1967), British Lieutenant-Colonel and intelligence officer during the later years of the Great Game or the Tournament of Shadows, the battle between the British and Russian Empires for supremacy in Central Asia. Born in Lahore, India, he trained as a professional soldier in England and served in the First World War before setting out on his famous mission to Tashkent to discover the intentions of the new Bolshevik government towards India. A master of many languages, both Eastern and Western, Bailey was also a fine horseman and an accomplished natural historian.

Nicolas de Basily, Russian diplomat 1903–17. Born into a noble family, he was educated largely abroad. His memoirs, which he wrote in French, remain an important historical source. After 1910, his work mostly concerned Russian strategic interests in Constantinople (now Istanbul) and the Turkish Straits. A trained lawyer, Basily drafted the document of abdication for Tsar Nicholas II.

Andrei Bely (1880–1934), *nom de plume* of Boris Nikolaevich Bugaev, poet, literary theorist and author of the famous novel *Petersburg*. Born into a prominent intellectual family in Moscow, he was part of the Symbolist movement and latterly an anthroposophist and friend of Rudolf Steiner. Bely died at Maximilian Voloshin's haven for writers and artists in Koktebel on the Black Sea.

Alexandr Blok (1880–1921), Symbolist poet. His family were St Petersburg intellectuals but after his parents' separation he was brought up by aristocratic relatives near Moscow. His youthful work was influenced by the Romantic lyric poets Fyodor Tyutchev and Afanasy Fet, and he was also drawn to the syncretic religious philosophy of Vladimir Solovyov. Blok was a close friend and mentor of the poet Anna Akhmatova. His later work focused on political themes, his short-lived enthusiasm for the Revolution being expressed in his 1918 poem *The Twelve*. Blok died in St Petersburg and is buried in the Smolensk cemetery.

Louise Bryant (1885–1936), American Marxist journalist. Like her husband, John Reed, she published an eyewitness account of the October revolution of 1917 in Petrograd. She died in France of a brain tumour.

Valery Bryusov (1873–1924), poet, prose writer, translator and author of a famous diary (1893–1905). Born into a Moscow merchant family, he became a leading figure in the Russian Symbolist movement and editor of the influential literary magazine *Vesy* (The Balance). Though sceptical about the Revolution, he accepted a formal position in the Ministry of Culture under the Bolshevik regime.

Mikhail Bulgakov (1891–1940), playwright, humourist and novelist, author of the posthumously published *The Master and Margarita*, a highly regarded satirical novel about the Soviet Union. Born in Kiev into a large and conspicuously happy family, his father a professor at the theological academy and his mother a teacher, he attended the local grammar school before training as a medical doctor at the St Vladimir University in Kiev. He served as an army physician in the First World War, during which he was badly wounded, and in the Civil War. Weakened by typhus, in 1919 he abandoned medicine to devote himself to literature and moved to Moscow, where he supported himself largely by journalism. Though protected by Stalin, Bulgakov soon ran afoul of the authorities. Although not physically persecuted, after the culturally vibrant 1920s he was denied publication and forbidden to emigrate. He died of an inherited kidney disease and is buried in Moscow.

Anton Chekhov (1860–1904), dramatist and short-story writer, author of several of Russia's most famous plays, including *Uncle Vanya* and *The Cherry Orchard*. Born in the port of Taganrog on the Sea of Asov in southern Russia, he spent most of his adult life in Moscow and on his estate of Melikhovo in the nearby countryside. Though a professional writer from his youth, Chekhov was also a trained doctor and he later provided free medical treatment for the peasants near his estate. In 1890, he undertook an important journey to the penal colony of Sakhalin island to gather census information. Chekhov died of tuberculosis in the Black Forest spa town of Badenweiler. He is buried in Moscow.

Marquis Astolphe de Custine (1790–1857), diplomat and travel writer, 'the de Tocqueville of Russia'. He was born into a wealthy and aristocratic family in Lorraine. His father and grandfather were both guillotined in the Terror, and Custine was raised by his intellectual mother and her lover, the great conservative Romantic writer Chateaubriand. His promising diplomatic career cut short by a public scandal over his homosexuality, Custine wrote a series of unsuccessful novels, poems and one play before finding his true vocation as a travel writer. His *Lettres de Russie* of 1839, deeply critical of the repressive regime of Tsar Nicholas I, was banned in Russia itself and not fully published there until 1996, but it enjoyed great success elsewhere in Europe. In English it was published as *Empire of the Tsar: A Journey through Eternal Russia*. A close friend of Balzac and Chopin, Custine lived most of his later life with his English companion, Edward Saint-Barbe.

Anna Dostoevsky (1846–1918), second wife of Fyodor Dostoevsky and author of an important diary and memoir of her life with the great writer. Born Anna Snitkina in St Petersburg, the daughter of a Ukrainian surveyor and his Finnish–Swedish wife, she trained as a stenographer and worked as Dostoevsky's secretary before marrying him in 1867. After their marriage, she continued to assist him, recording the day's work, which he dictated to her each evening. The couple had three children. On Dostoevsky's death in 1881, Anna devoted herself to the perpetuation of his memory, founding the Dostoevsky Museum in St Petersburg, publishing new editions of his work and compiling a bibliographical index of it. Anna Dostoevsky died in desperate circumstances in Yalta, destitute, cut off from her family by military action following the Revolution and weakened by malaria and semi-starvation.

Fyodor Dostoevsky (1821–81), author of psychological realist masterpieces including *Crime and Punishment* and *The Brothers Karamazov*. Born in Moscow into the minor nobility, he was introduced by his parents to the riches of Russian literature. Educated first at a French academy and then at a prestigious grammar school in Moscow, he later studied military engineering in St Petersburg. His first novel, *Poor Folk*, published when Dostoevsky was just 26, was well received. At the age of 28, however, owing to his friendship with members of the Petrashevsky Circle, he was arrested, subjected to a mock execution and sentenced to four years' hard labour and six subsequent years of exile in Siberia. He eventually returned to St Petersburg and a writing life of great brilliance. In later life, Dostoevsky suffered from pulmonary emphysema. He died of a lung haemorrhage and was buried at the Alexander Nevsky Monastery in St Petersburg.

Vladimir Gilyarovsky (1853–1935), writer and journalist, a larger-than-life character of great humour and immense physical strength, best known for his memoirs of Moscow at the turn of the twentieth century. He came from a modest family in the northwestern town of Vologda and enjoyed an adventurous boyhood before running away to become a barge-hauler on the Volga. A series of challenging and colourful jobs followed - firefighter, horse herder, soldier, circus rider, actor - before he settled into journalism. Encouraged by his close friend Anton Chekhov, in 1887 Gilyarovsky produced his first book, *People of the Slums*, which detailed the desperate lives of Moscow's poor, but the book was destroyed by the authorities. Gilyarovsky continued sympathetically to document the city's underworld of poverty and crime, earning the affectionate nickname 'Uncle Gilyai'. He died in Moscow

Nikolai Gogol (1809–52), realist and surrealist fiction writer and playwright. Born into a minor gentry family of Ukrainian Cossack extraction in Velyki Sorochyntsi (now in Ukraine), he worked in St Petersburg as a bureaucrat and briefly as a professor of history before turning to literature. His most famous works include the comic novel *Dead Souls* and short stories *The Nose* and *The Overcoat*. He lived a great deal abroad, mostly in Rome. In middle age, Gogol fell prey to an increasing religious mania. He returned to Russia and, convinced by his spiritual director

of the sinfulness of his writing, he destroyed the second part of *Dead Souls*, and died after subjecting himself to a regime of severe fasting.

Maxim Gorky (1868–1936) *nom de plume* of Alexei Maximovich Peshkov, prose writer, dramatist and political activist. His works describe the lives of the poor and the marginalized in Russian society. Born in Nizhny Novgorod, he travelled widely in the Empire, working as a journalist, before settling in Moscow. His activism against the Tsarist regime earned him several spells in prison, and he spent two long periods, both before and after the 1917 Revolution, of voluntary exile in Italy. Though a Bolshevik and a friend of both Lenin and Stalin, Gorky was critical of the new regime, and it is thought he may have been murdered on Stalin's orders.

Alexander Herzen (1812–70), publisher and memoirist. Born in Moscow to a Russian nobleman and his German *de facto* wife, he studied mathematics and physical sciences at Moscow University and served several years in political exile in the provinces before establishing himself in St Petersburg as a journalist and prominent member of the radical intelligentsia. At the age of 35, he inherited a fortune and set off on a lengthy European journey, never to return to Russia. From London, he published *The Pole Star* and, with his friend Nikolay Ogaryev, *The Bell*, revolutionary periodicals in the Russian language, as well as his famous memoir, *My Past and Thoughts*. Though a passionate socialist, Herzen was sceptical of abstract ideologies, preferring to focus on practical, attainable reforms. He died in political exile in London.

Marina de Heyden (1889–1969), author of a memoir of the latter days of the Tsarist regime and the Revolution. A Russian countess of partly Dutch extraction, daughter of a naval *aide-de-camp* to Tsar Nicholas II, she enjoyed a luxurious upbringing and was a frequent visitor to the imperial court. In 1909, although in love with Prince Nicholas Yusupov, she was married against her will to Count Arvid Manteuffel. The love triangle resulted in a duel between the two men, in which Yusupov was shot dead. Her health impaired, Marina spent three months in a Finnish sanatorium and she and Manteuffel were divorced. After the Revolution, the de Heyden family went into exile in France, where Marina was to live for the rest of her life. She was briefly married to Michael Chichagov, with whom she had a son in 1920.

Alexander Kerensky (1881–1970), second Premier of the Provisional Government following the abdication of Tsar Nicholas II in March 1917. He was born in Simbirsk (now Ulyanovsk) some 550 miles east of Moscow. His father was a school principal and his mother from a wealthy and well-connected family. Kerensky's father's work soon took the family to Tashkent, where the boy attended the local grammar school before moving to St Petersburg to study law. He subsequently gained a reputation for his defence of revolutionaries in political trials. Elected to the Duma in 1912, Kerensky pursued a moderate socialist course. Outmanoeuvred by Lenin, he fell from power after the October Revolution of 1917. Kerensky went into exile first in Paris and eventually in the US. He died in New York, but local Orthodox churches refused to conduct funeral rites for him and he was buried in London.

Mikhail Lermontov (1814–41), Romantic writer, 'poet of the Caucasus', descendant of George Learmont, a Scottish officer who entered Russian service in the seventeenth century. Born in Moscow into a noble military family, he suffered poor health and was taken at the age of 10 to the milder Caucasus, a region to which he retained a strong attachment. He returned to Moscow to attend grammar school and, briefly, university, before moving to St Petersburg to train as a guards officer. In his work, Lermontov was critical of what he perceived as the vicious and self-serving values of the Russian aristocracy, and he was soon transferred back to the Caucasus on military duty. Known for his sharp and often insulting wit, Lermontov was shot dead by a fellow officer in a duel in Piatigorsk. He was only 27.

Sir R. H. Bruce Lockhart (1887–1970), diplomat, secret agent, writer and broadcaster. Born in the Scottish town of Anstruther in Fife into a family of schoolmasters, he was educated at Fettes College in Edinburgh before spending three years in Malaya managing his uncle's rubber plantation. While there, Lockhart began writing short stories and poems. He also created a scandal by living openly with a Malayan princess, ward of the local Sultan. In 1912, Lockhart was appointed British Vice-Consul in Moscow; he was to remain in Russia until after the Revolution, subsequently serving the British Legation in the new republic of Czechoslovakia. During the 1920s, he was charged with increasing the influence of British banks in Central Europe. On his return to London, he became an editor for the *Evening Standard* newspaper. During the Second World War, he was supervisor of press and radio propaganda in liaison with MI6. Lockhart was knighted in 1943. He died in Scotland.

Osip Mandelstam (1891–1938), poet. Born in Warsaw and educated at the prestigious Tenishev school in St Petersburg, he travelled and studied for several years in western Europe before returning to Russia to study philology. Influenced by Nikolay Gumilyov, first husband of the poet Anna Akhmatova, he became active in the Acmeist movement, publishing poems of precision and 'this-worldliness', in contrast to the 'other-worldliness' of the Symbolists. Mandelstam was arrested during the purges of 1938 and died in a transit camp near Vladivostok.

Vladimir Nabokov (1899–1977), writer and professor of Russian literature. Born in St Petersburg to an intellectual aristocratic family, he left Russia after the Revolution and studied at Trinity College, Cambridge, before joining his family in Berlin. Nabokov published his first literary work, in Russian, while still in his twenties. In 1940, he moved to the United States to begin an academic career, first at Wellesley College and later at Cornell University. He won great fame with his English-language novels and his autobiography *Speak, Memory* and in 1973, he was awarded the American National Medal for Literature. Nabokov died in Montreux, Switzerland.

Maurice Paléologue (1859–1944), diplomat, historian and writer. His family were cultured and aristocratic Romanian *émigrés* who settled in Paris. Paléologue attended the prestigious Henri-IV and Louis-le-Grand lycées before taking a degree in law. In 1880, he joined the French Ministry of Foreign Affairs, serving in Europe, North Africa and China before his appointment as Ambassador to the imperial Russian court in 1914. The diary which he kept during his three years at St Petersburg remains an important historical source for the Russian conduct of the First World War and the last days of the Empire. Alongside his diplomatic career, Paléologue was active in literary circles, contributing to *La Revue des deux mondes* and writing novels and essays of his own. In 1928, he was elected a member of the Académie Française. Paléologue died in Paris shortly after the city's liberation towards the end of the Second World War.

Boris Pasternak (1890–1960), poet, translator and novelist. Born into a cultured and intellectual Moscow family, he was educated by his parents and private tutors before entering the Fifth Moscow Gymnasium, where he acquired a predominantly classical education. Inspired by Alexander Scriabin, a close family friend, the young Pasternak at first studied music and especially composition, but in 1909 he began studying law and then philosophy at Moscow University and in Marburg, Germany. By the age of 20, he was also writing poetry. Initially strongly influenced by the symbolism of Alexandr Blok, Pasternak gradually developed a markedly independent lyrical style. Though primarily a poet, Pasternak is best known outside Russia for his novel *Doctor Zhivago*, for which he was awarded (and obliged to refuse) the Nobel Prize in 1958. The Nobel committee was later revealed to have been manipulated by the British and American secret services in order to embarrass the Soviet government. Despite pressure from the authorities, Pasternak resisted exile to the West. He died of lung cancer in the village of Peredelkino near Moscow.

Alexander Pushkin (1799–1837), widely acknowledged as the progenitor of modern Russian literature, in prose as well as in his better-known genre of poetry, with a commensurate influence on the modern Russian language itself. His best-known work is perhaps the novel in verse *Eugene Onegin*. Born into the Moscow nobility, he was educated at the Imperial Lyceum in Tsarskoye Selo, near St Petersburg, now named Pushkin in his honour. Pushkin's liberal political views forced him into exile in the Caucasus, where his quiet support of atheism subsequently led to his house arrest for two years. A frequent dueller, he died of a gunshot wound sustained in his 19th duel. He is buried near Pskov.

John Reed (1887–1920), Harvard-educated American journalist sympathetic to the Bolsheviks. The husband of journalist Louise Bryant, he is today best remembered for his eyewitness account of the October Revolution of 1917. He died of typhus in Moscow and is buried in the Heroes' Grave in Red Square.

Fyodor Sologub (1863–1927), *nom de plume* of Fedor Kuzmic Teternikov. Symbolist novelist and poet. Born in St Petersburg in poor circumstances, his father a tailor and former serf and his mother an illiterate servant, Sologub trained at the St Petersburg Teachers' Institute and worked as a teacher and school inspector for 25 years, writing in his spare time. Though sometimes sensationalist and often controversial, his work was highly regarded, and as a writer Sologub was frequently compared to Gogol. Despite his anti-Bolshevik stance, he held posts in the St Petersburg Union of Writers after the Revolution and his work continued to be published. He died an acclaimed writer and translator in the city of his birth.

Alfred Lord Tennyson (1809–1892), lyric and narrative poet. Born in Lincolnshire into a well-to-do rector's family, he was educated at local grammar schools and at Trinity College, Cambridge. Together with two of his brothers, he published a first collection of poems at the age of 17. A favoured poet of Queen Victoria, Tennyson became Poet Laureate on Wordsworth's death in 1850. In 1884, the first writer to be so honoured, he was raised to the baronetcy and took a seat in the House of Lords. *The Charge of the Light Brigade*, one of his best-known works, narrates the drama of a doomed British cavalry charge against Russian forces during the Crimean War Battle of Balaclava on 25 October 1854. Tennyson continued writing poetry into his old age. He is buried in Westminster Abbey in London.

Leo Tolstoy (1828–1910), realist novelist, author of *War and Peace* and *Anna Karenina*. Born on his aristocratic family's estate of Yasnaya Polyana in the Tula region south of Moscow, he studied briefly at Kazan University before joining the army and serving in the Crimean War, subsequently returning to Yasnaya Polyana. In later life he became committed to an ascetic and pacifist Christianity. Having determined to leave his estate and live as a poor wanderer, Tolstoy fell mortally ill at a nearby railway station. He is buried at Yasnaya Polyana.

Count Sergei Witte (1849–1915), Finance Minister and later Premier of Imperial Russia. Born in Tiflis, then administrative centre of the viceroyalty of the Caucasus, where his father held an important civil service post, he was privately educated before enrolling as a mathematics student at the new Novorossiysk University in Odessa. Aided by an influential uncle, he then began a career in the burgeoning railways industry, also writing political articles for a progressive local newspaper. In 1888, after some 15 years working for private companies in Kiev and St Petersburg, Witte became Director of State Railways. Subsequently, as Finance Minister and Premier, he instigated important economic reforms, at the same time supporting plans for territorial expansion in the far east of the Empire. This work on both these fronts gained him the enmity of conservatives within the government and among private landowners, and in 1906 he was forced into retirement. His celebrated memoirs were first published, in English, in 1921.

LITERARY SOURCES

Anna Akhmatova, in Dimitri Obolensky (ed.), *The Heritage of Russian Verse*. Bloomington, IN: Indiana University Press, 1965.

Alexandra, Tsarina, and Nicholas, Tsar II, *A Lifelong Passion: The Letters of Nicholas and Alexandra*. London: Doubleday, 1997.

Alexandra, Tsarina, *The Last Diary*, ed. Robert K. Massie. New Haven, CT: Yale University Press, 1997.

Anonymous, *Confession sexuelle d'un anonyme russe (Collection: Lectures amoureuses de Jean-Jacques Pauvert)*. Paris: Editions La Musardine, 1997.

F. M. Bailey, *Mission to Tashkent*. London: The Folio Society, 1999.

Nicolas de Basily, *Memoirs*. Stanford, CA: Hoover Institution Press, Stanford University, 1973.

Andrei Bely, *Petersburg*, trans. Robert A. Maguire and John E. Malmstad. Bloomington, IN, and London: Indiana University Press, 1978.

Alexandr Blok, *Selected Poems*. Moscow: Progress Publishers, 1981.

Louise Bryant, *Six Red Months in Russia: An Observer's Account of Russia Before and During the Proletarian Dictatorship*. New York: George H. Doran Company, 1918.

Valery Bryusov, *The Diary (1893–1905), with reminiscences by V. F. Khodasevich and Marina Tsvetaeva*, ed. and trans. Joan Delaney Grossman. Berkeley and Los Angeles, CA: University of California Press, 1980.

Mikhail Bulgakov, *Manuscripts Don't Burn: A Life in Letters and Diaries*, trans. and ed. J. A. E. Curtis. London: Bloomsbury, 1991.

Anton Chekhov, *Die Vaterlosen [Platonov]*, trans. and publ. Peter Urban. Zürich: Diogenes, 1995; known in English as *That Worthless Fellow Platonov* or simply *Platonov*.

Anton Chekhov, *Five Plays*, trans. Ronald Hingley. Oxford: Oxford University Press, 1980.

Anton Chekhov, *Anton Chekhov's Life and Thought: Selected Letters*, trans. Michael Henry Heim with commentary by Simon Karlinsky. Berkeley and Los Angeles, CA: University of California Press, 1975.

Maria Chekhova, *Mein Bruder Anton Tschechow [My Brother Anton Chekhov]*. Berlin: Kindler, 2004.

Astolphe de Custine, Marquis, *Lettres de Russie*, recorded and presented by Henri Massis. Paris: Livre Club du Librairie, 1960.

Anna Dostoevsky, *Dostoevsky: Reminiscences*, trans. and ed. Beatrice Stillman. New York: Liveright, 1975.

Fyodor Dostoevsky, *Notes from the Dead House*, trans. Guy and Elena Cook. Moscow: Raduga Publishers, 1989.

Vladimir Gilyarovsky (Wladimir Giljarowski), *Moskau und die Moskauer [Moscow and the Muscovites]*. Minsk: Verlag Höchste Schule.

Nikolai Gogol, 'Nevsky Prospect', in *The Collected Tales of Nikolai Gogol*, trans. and ed. Richard Pevear and Larissa Volokhonsky. London: Granta Books, 2003.

Maxim Gorky, *Gorky's Tolstoy and other Reminiscences: Key writings by and about Maxim Gorky*, trans. and ed. Donald Fanger. New Haven, CT, and London: Yale University Press, 2008.

Alexander Herzen, *My Past and Thoughts*, trans. Constance Garnett. Berkeley, Los Angeles, CA, and London: University of California Press, 1973.

Marina de Heyden, *Les rubis portent malheur: au crépuscule d'une cour*. Monte Carlo: Editions Regain, 1967.

Alexander Kerensky, *The Kerensky Memoirs: Russia and History's Turning Point*. London: Cassell, 1966.

Mikhail Lermontov, in Dimitri Obolensky (ed.), *The Heritage of Russian Verse*, Bloomington, IN: Indiana University Press, 1965.

R. H. Bruce Lockhart, *Memoirs of a British Agent*. London: Folio, 2003.

Osip Mandelstam, *Stone*, trans. Robert Tracy. London: Harvill Press, 1997.

Vladimir Mayakovsky, *Love is the Heart of Everything: Correspondence between Vladimir Mayakovsky and Lili Brik 1915–1930*, ed. Bengt Jangfeldt. New York: Grove Press, 1986.

Vladimir Nabokov, *Speak, Memory: An Autobiography Revisited*. London: Weidenfeld and Nicolson, 1967 (revised ed.).

Nicholas II, Tsar, *Journal intime*, trans. A. Pierre. Paris: Payot, 1925.

Dimitri Obolensky (ed.), *The Heritage of Russian Verse*. Bloomington, IN: Indiana University Press, 1965.

Maurice Paléologue, *La Russie des Tsars pendant la Grande Guerre*, 3 vols. Paris: Plon, 1922.

Boris Pasternak, *Doctor Zhivago*, trans. Manya Harari and Max Hayward. London: Everyman, 1958.

Boris Pasternak, *Selected Poems*, trans. Jon Stallworthy and Peter France. London: Penguin, 1984.

Alexander Pushkin, *Selected Poems*, trans. D. M. Thomas. London: Penguin, 1983.

John Reed, *Ten Days That Shook the World*. London: Penguin, 1977.

Fyodor Sologub, *The Petty Demon*, trans. S. D. Cioran. Aylesbury, Buckinghamshire: Quartet Books, 1990.

Alfred, Lord Tennyson, *The Works of Alfred Lord Tennyson*. London: Wordsworth Editions, 1994.

Leo Tolstoy, *Anna Karenina*, trans. Rosemary Edmonds. London: Penguin, 1978.

Leo Tolstoy, *The Cossacks*, trans. Louise and Aylmer Maude. London: Everyman, 1994.

Sergei Witte, Count, *The Memoirs*, trans. and ed. Sidney Harcave. Armonk, NY, and London: M. E. Sharpe, Inc., 1990.

PHOTOGRAPHIC SOURCES

a. = above, b. = below, l. = left, r. = right, m. = middle

Beinecke Rare Book and Manuscript Library, Yale University, New Haven, CT: pages 4 (second from top), 15 a., 45, 48 (2), 49, 50 (3), 51, 52, 53, 174; Ghetto Fighters House Archive: page 111; Andrew Howe: pages 33 a., 37 a., 215 (2), 217 a., 222 b., 222/223, 224 b., 225, 238 b., 238/239; Imagno / Austrian Archives, Vienna: pages 2, 4 b., 5 (second and fifth from top), 6/7, 10/11, 15 b., 18 r.a., 18 r.b., 19, 21, 23, 25, 26/27, 36 a., 38, 39 r.a., 40 a., 42/43, 44 r., 46 l.b., 47, 55 b., 57, 62 (2), 72, 73 a., 88, 89, 90 b., 92 l.a., 92 r.m., 100/101, 101 b., 103 b., 105, 106, 114 b., 115 b., 116 (2), 118 a., 120, 126 b., 127, 128, 129, 139, 154, 155, 156 (3), 156/157, 161 a., 164, 165, 166, 169 (3), 170 b., 175 l.b., 175 a., 177, 181 (2), 187 b., 197, 198, 201, 206/207, 210/211, 212 a., 212 b., 213, 214, 216 (2), 217 b., 218, 219 (2), 220, 221 (3), 222 a., 224 a., 226 (2), 226/227, 228, 229, 231 b., 232 (2), 233, 234, 235 (3), 236, 237 b., 238 a., 240 (2), 241, 242/243, 243; Imagno / Photoinstitut Bonartes: pages 8/9, 34, 36 a., 42 b., 56, 85 (2), 104, 115 a., 132 b., 135, 171 b., 172 b., 200; Imagno / Franz Hubmann: pages 87 r.a., 92 r.a., 92 r.b., 110 (2); Imagno / ÖNB: page 55 a.; Imagno / Ullsteinbild: pages 31, 32, 33 l.b., 33 r.b., 35 m., 40 b., 46 a., 54 (2), 63, 172 b.; Wikipedia / Sergey Lvovich Levitsky: page 18 l.; Keystone Mast: pages 73 l.b., 94 b., 98, 101 a., 102, 103 r.a., 117 (2), 118 b. (2), 159 r.; Leeds University: pages 80, 81 (4), 82/83; Library of Congress, Prints and Photographs Division, Washington, DC, Armenian Relief Committee: pages 132 a., 133 r.; Library of Congress, Prints and Photographs Division, Washington, DC, Bain Collection: pages 41, 44 l., 46 r.b.; Library of Congress, Prints and Photographs Division, Washington, DC, Carpenter Collection: pages 87 l.a., 87 u; Library of Congress, Prints and Photographs Division, Washington, DC, Photochrom Prints: pages 4 (fifth from top), 24 (2), 27, 42 a., 84/85, 94 a., 96 (2), 97, 99 (2), 107, 108 (2), 109, 122, 134 a., 137, 207 (2); Library of Congress, Prints and Photographs Division, Washington, DC, Prokudin-Gorkii Collection: pages 4 (fourth from top), 5 a., 5 (fourth from top), 5 b., 14, 58 (2), 58/59, 60, 61, 64 (2), 65, 66 (2), 67, 68/69, 69, 70, 71 (2), 73 r.b., 74, 75 (2), 76, 77, 78/79, 79, 86, 90 a., 103 l.a., 114 a., 121, 123, 124, 125 (2), 130 a., 130 l.b., 131, 136, 138, 140 (2), 141, 142, 143 (2), 144, 145, 146/147, 148/149, 149 (2), 150, 151 (2), 152, 153 (4), 167 m., 168/169, 176, 178/179, 179 (2), 180, 182, 183, 184, 185 (2), 186, 187 a., 188/189, 189 (2), 190 (2), 191, 192, 193, 194 (2), 195, 202, 203, 204, 205 (2); Library of Congress, Prints and Photographs Division, Washington, DC, Fenton Crimean War Photographs: pages 17, 112 (2); Library of Congress, Prints and Photographs Division, Washington, DC, Stereograph Cards: pages 93 r.a., 93 b., 162 a., 163; Library of Congress, Prints and Photographs Division, Washington, DC, George Kennan Papers: pages 16, 159 l., 161 b., 167 a.; Library of Congress, Prints and Photographs Division, Washington, DC, National Photo Company Collection: page 95; Library of Congress, Prints and Photographs Division, Washington, DC, Underwood & Underwood: pages 162 b., 175 r.b., 211; Mapping St Petersburg / www.petersburg.berkeley.edu: pages 35 l.a., 35 r.a., 35 l.b., 35 r.b.; Meyers Konversations-Lexikon, Band XVII. Sechste Auflage. Bibliographisches Institut: Leipzig und Wien 1906: pages 12/13; Nevsky Prospekt / www.nevsky-prospekt.com: pages 22, 29, 39 b.; Rosphoto, St Petersburg: pages 1 (third from top), 28/29, 30; Zeno, Berlin: pages 4 (second from top), 5 (third from top), 20, 37 b., 39 l.a., 91, 93 l.a., 113, 119, 126 a., 130 r.b., 133 l., 134 b., 146, 158, 160, 167 b., 170 a., 171 a., 172 a., 173, 196, 199, 208 (2), 209, 210, 211 a. (3), 237 a.

Many of the original colour photographs in this book were taken with an early camera that used three lenses with colour filters to register the red, yellow and blue spectrums sequentially on a photographic plate, with a fourth lens capturing the image in black and white. These four images were then superimposed and projected as a single picture. Any tiny movement in the scene between one image and the next created a ghosting effect in the final image.

ACKNOWLEDGMENTS

Prof. Dr Bert G. Fragner
Elisabeth Hölzl
Andrew M. Howe
Tanja Star-Busman

First published in the United Kingdom in 2013 by
Thames & Hudson Ltd, 181A High Holborn,
London WC1V 7QX

www.thamesandhudson.com

First published in 2013 in hardcover in the United States of America by
Thames & Hudson Inc., 500 Fifth Avenue, New York, New York 10110

thamesandhudsonusa.com

Original edition © 2012 by Christian Brandstätter Verlag, Vienna
This edition © 2013 Thames & Hudson, London

Picture design and layout by Philipp Blom, Christian Brandstätter
and Veronica Buckley

British Library Cataloguing-in-Publication Data
A catalogue record for this book is available from the British Library

Library of Congress Catalog Card Number 2012943633

ISBN: 978-0-500-51668-3

Printed and bound in China